What Would Shakespeare Do?

Personal Advice from the Bard

JESS WINFIELD

GRAMERCY BOOKS
NEW YORK

Quotes from Shakespeare's works are from *The Riverside Shakespeare*, G. Blakemore Evans (Editor), Copyright © 1974 by Houghton Mifflin Company. Used with permission.

The Riverside Shakespeare uses the "Through Line Numbers" as established by Charles Hinman in *The Norton Facsimile: The First Folio of Shakespeare* and in the *Norton Shakespeare*, and are Copyright © 1968 by W.W. Norton and Company, Inc. Used with permission

This 2002 edition published by Gramercy Books, an imprint of Random House Value Publishing, a division of Random House, Inc., 280 Park Avenue, New York, NY 10017, by arrangement with Ulysses Press, Berkeley, California.

Gramercy is a registered trademark and the colophon is a trademark of Random House, Inc.

Printed in the United States of America

Interior design: Leslie Henriques, Sarah Levin

Random House
New York • Toronto • London • Sydney • Auckland
www.randomhouse.com

A catalog record for this title is available from the Library of Congress

ISBN: 0-517-22006-7

9 8 7 6 5 4 3 2 1

For Sa—
the best decision I've ever made

Acknowledgements

It is a rare gift for a writer to be *asked* to write a book at all, much less about a subject so near and dear to his heart. But this project has been a true joy; I've learned much about Shakespeare in the process, but more about myself. So, I first and foremost thank Ray Riegert and Leslie Henriques for believing I had both the character and the Shakespearean chops to tackle such a weighty subject, and for bringing Shakespeare back front and center when I threatened to upstage him. Thanks also to Bryce Willett, Claire Chun, Steven Schwartz, and Sarah Fahey at Ulysses Press for their patience with me as I went slowly mad with the looming deadline.

I also thank my good friends Franz Metcalf and Philip Abrams. Without them, this book would never have come to be, or would have been written by someone else. For past encouragement and nurturing of my love for the Bard, I'll list Amy Reed, Randy Stewart, Virginia Gangsei, Daniel Singer, Adam Long, and, if he only knew how much, Tom Stoppard. I'd also like to thank Hugh Richmond of the University of California at Berkeley, who has greatly influenced my interpretation of the Bard's works. Oh, and thanks to Tom Scoville (whom I forgot to thank in my last book) for two very funny jokes.

Mostly, I'd like to thank my close friends and family, who have been so understanding while I disappeared physically and emotionally to write this book. Erika, Will, Jack, Hazel, Q, Shelley, Hughes ... I can come out and play now!

The same in spades goes for Sa, "my wife" of these pages, whose own practical wisdom is reflected throughout, and whose support and tolerance over the last months have been above and beyond what even Shakespeare would do.

Finally, I thank William Shakespeare himself, for "being there" for me. And, as always, special thanks to Greg Moore.

The Shakespearean text in the following pages is taken from the the still-unsurpassed *The Riverside Shakespeare* text of the Complete Works (1974 edition), although I have occasionally modernized spelling and punctuation as the whim suits me. The line numbers also refer to that edition; the actual mileage of your own edition may vary.

Character names are cited for the quotes, except when the character speaking is the same as the title of the play.

Table of Contents

Introduction

In years past, various authors have written reams of self-help material based on the question, "What would Jesus do?" Another author, and a dear friend of mine, has recently considered "What would Buddha do?" Still others (the creators of *South Park*, for those of you whose interests don't stretch from Shakespeare to R-rated cartoons) ask, "What would Brian Boitano do?"

Although I hope there's nothing in here to offend Christians, Buddhists, or figure-skating aficionados, the slender volume you now hold is intended to add a slightly more literary, secular, and humanist angle to the discussion. It encourages you, when faced with a difficult decision in your life, to pause for a moment and ask yourself: "What would Shakespeare do?" My hope is that, by consciously getting "inside the head" of the great Bard, we might draw out of ourselves the qualities he champions: practicality, compassion, humility, generosity, honesty, and tolerance.

As a starting point, I've posed a hundred or so everyday dilemmas, ranging from the trivial to the essential, from the ethical to the moral, from the personal to the political, and supplied answers from the Bard's works that try to suggest what he might do if faced with the same circumstances. And oh yeah, there's also a bunch of commentary by yours truly. More about that later.

Before we dig in to the literary/self-help feast that awaits you, let us first set the table.

Who Was William Shakespeare?

You've probably heard at least one of these theories:

1. William Shakespeare was Francis Bacon.

2. William Shakespeare was Christopher Marlowe.

3. William Shakespeare was Edward DeVere, the 17th Earl of Oxford.

4. If you put a monkey at a typewriter for long enough, he'd eventually type the complete works of William Shakespeare.

Of those theories, number four is the only one with any hard evidence to back it up.

Let's get this straight right now. William Shakespeare was William Shakespeare. I don't have time to go into the scholarly whys and wherefores, but please trust me: for anyone else to have been William Shakespeare would have required an Elizabethan cover-up conspiracy the size, complexity, and unlikelihood of which would dwarf all the most paranoid JFK, Roswell, and Elvis conspiracies combined. My advice when anyone tells you Shakespeare was anybody besides humble William from Stratford? Smile politely, tell them you hear the phone ringing in the next room, slip out and call the funny farm. They're either ignorant on the issue or a danger to themselves and others.

The truth is this. William Shakespeare was born in 1564 in the prosperous but provincial English town of Stratford-upon-Avon. After a seemingly quiet small-town childhood, he married young, had two kids, and vanished for about ten years. (I vanished at about age 18 too ... I can just imagine all the trouble Will was getting into!) He re-emerged as an up-and-coming actor and playwright in the burgeoning London theater scene of Queen Elizabeth I's reign. It's a pretty typical story: artistic young wag shakes the small town dust off his boots, goes to the big city, spends some time playing bit parts and honing his craft, and finally breaks into the big time. After writing an incredible 37 plays, 150 sonnets and three long poems (that we know of) in a brief 20-year career—during which he also became a businessman and part owner of the theater company he worked in—Shakespeare retired back to Stratford, where he lived out his remaining years quietly. He died in 1616 at the age of 52.

Why William Shakespeare?

If his life was so unexceptional, then why, today, should we care what Shakespeare would do?

On one level, William Shakespeare was simply a practical and highly successful individual whose works happen to contain a highly quotable wealth of proverbs, aphorisms, and plain-talk advice about the little things in life.

Then there's the whole Immortal-Bard-of-the-Ages angle. Whether it was hard work, divine inspiration, a rare flowering of human genius, or just an extraordinary vindication of the monkey-at-a-typewriter theory, William Shakespeare was simply unsurpassed at probing and illuminating the human condition with depth and compassion and translating his insights into memorable poetry and powerful theater. His characters are so astutely drawn, so essentially human, so timeless, that they work as well for modern theater audiences as they did in baroque French courts or rowdy Old West revues. We can only imagine how they played to Shakespeare's intended Elizabethan audiences, who would understand every contemporary historical reference and obscure slang pun! The Bard's works are so universal that they're equally effective when transposed to the Japanese cinema (check out *Throne of Blood*,

Akira Kurosawa's adaptation of *Macbeth*), Italian opera (Verdi's *Otello*), or American musical (*Kiss Me, Kate; West Side Story*).

Shakespeare's influence on our culture has been so profound that, in a very real sense, we have actually become *products* of his work. We think that a young lover speaking to her beau from a balcony is romantic because of Shakespeare's *Romeo and Juliet*. We know that jealousy is a green-eyed monster because of *Othello*. We believe that all's well that ends well because Shakespeare said so. Shakespeare's art was so prodigious that it not only held "the mirror up to nature," offering a true reflection of life, but it actually *created* nature: turns of phrase, attitudes, character types, all traceable back to Shakespeare's creative power. When you think of it this way, it's not surprising that Will Shakespeare, humble actor and playwright, was recently voted the third-most influential person of the last millenium.

So really, where better to seek personal advice than in the works of William Shakespeare, a man who has not only depicted us as we are and as we wish we were, but who has had a hand in actually *making* us who we are?

The Problem With This Book

I'm here to act as a kind of medium—a go-between from your daily problems to the Bard's wisdom. You have a question; I answer with Shakespeare's voice.

But let's be honest: I'm just guessing. Educated guesses, perhaps, but who really knows what the historical William Shakespeare, prowling the London theater district or strolling the Stratford countryside in his breeches and doublet, would have done about *anything* in his own life?

What kind of tea did he like? Was he kind to small animals? Who knows? Unlike the subjects of similar advice books (such as *What Would Jesus Do?* or *What Would Buddha Do?*), Shakespeare wasn't a figure of adoration and worship during his lifetime. His actions weren't chronicled by devout disciples. We don't even know for certain what religion, if any, he professed. He was a secular businessman, whose business happened to be the theater and whose plays have survived the test of time. It is through Shakespeare's works, not his deeds, that we know and respect him.

Even in those works, Shakespeare didn't formulate a system of belief and ritual meant to be precisely followed by priests and monks. His plays contain no Ten Commandments or Four Noble Truths. They contain only settings, scene numbers, stage directions ... and the utterings of a vast multitude of *characters*. There are good characters and bad characters, generous characters and stingy characters, brash characters and meek characters. There are wise characters who come to horrible ends, and foolish characters who come out just fine.

This causes some difficulty for the type of book at hand. The word of Jesus is gospel, and every utterance of his speaks directly to his doctrine of love, salvation, the Kingdom of God. But Shakespeare's not nearly so single-minded. If you were to ask, "What would Shakespeare do about giving to the poor?" I could choose to answer with a quote from *Timon of Athens*: "Hate all, curse all, show charity to none!" Is that really what Shakespeare would do? Of course not. It merely reflects how Timon, a tragically flawed character, feels in specific circumstances at that instant in the play. Clearly, the answers you'll get to the question "What would Shakespeare do?" depend a lot on who is picking the quote. So beware! "The devil," as the Bard warns us, "may quote Scripture for his purpose." Which brings us to...

Why Jess Winfield?

I hope you won't come away from this book thinking that *I'm* the devil, quoting the Bard for my purpose! But let me be perfectly clear here: the opinions, prejudices, and hang-ups of Jess Winfield are totally reflected in these pages. Now, I know that if you're facing a dilemma large or small and you look to this book for help, you damn well want to know what wisdom *the Bard*, not Jess Winfield, has to offer. During the course of researching this book, reading between the lines in pursuit of the real William Shakespeare, I feel like I caught a glimpse of the man behind the quill pen. I've tried, whenever possible, to sort through the issues of character and situation, circumstance and rhetoric, to share that glimpse with you and offer advice that I feel genuinely represents what the historical Bard might have offered.

Nevertheless, at times, this book subtly (or not-so-subtly) transforms into "What Would Jess Winfield Do? ... as illustrated by the words of William Shakespeare." In fact, my choice of quotes from Shakespeare's works and my subsequent commentary will probably tell you as much about me as about Shakespeare. But I figured the advice from the Bard I chose to pass along would inevitably reflect my own taste, so I might as well be up front about it. At the very least, I've tried to warn you when I'm veering off the road of Shakespearean wisdom and rolling into the shallow drainage ditch of Winfield-y platitude.

Since I do offer some of my own advice in the following pages, you should know a few things: I'm not particularly religious, I have no training in psychology or social work, I've never raised a child, and I've got plenty of personal quirks and character flaws. I'm not even a Shakespeare scholar. In fact—big confession time—there are still one or two of his plays I've never seen or read!

But if this book has an overarching theme, it is that the spirit of humanity, which Shakespeare captured so beautifully in his works, resides in each of us. Whether bard or banker, poet or pawnbroker, playwright or politician, we all share one world, and its comedies, tragedies, and histories make us laugh, cry, and reflect as one. Awareness of this leads to tolerance and compassion, which leads to the understanding of others, which finally leads to the ultimate knowledge: of ourselves. And from self-knowledge is born integrity, honesty, duty, humility ... all of the great virtues Shakespeare espouses.

Maybe I'm not the best-qualified person to be offering up a book of personal advice, or even a book about Shakespeare, but I suspect that the Bard would say that I'm a human being, and therefore just as good a choice as anyone. I think he'd say that I should offer my book in a spirit of generosity, speak the truth as I understand it, and fear the judgment of no man ... no, nor woman, neither.

Yes ... I suspect that's exactly what Shakespeare would do.

O Brave New World!

I often wonder what someone from the distant past would think of our modern life, if he or she were suddenly plopped down in the middle of it. Fast cars, loud music, big-screen TV, the Internet, rollercoasters, hip-hop fashion, Super Bowl Sunday … would any of it make any sense? Perhaps not. But then, sometimes it doesn't make sense to those of us who live in it either.

Modern life can be overwhelming. We work long hours, maybe at two jobs, we have shopping to do, homes to keep, junk mail to dispose of. And the joy of modern telecommunications forces us to make snap decisions about it all in the blink of an eye or the click of a mouse. It's tough, with all that 3-D Dolby THX real-life input blazing around us, to remember to live our daily lives with some balance, and maybe a little bit of kindness.

Many people never come to appreciate the wisdom Shakespeare has to offer because they find him too foreign; his language and culture seem so different from our own. So in this first section of the book, let's begin with baby steps and see if we can get to know the Bard on our own turf, by applying his wisdom to some of the endless small, practical difficulties of our daily lives. Some of these may seem trivial. But keep in mind that Shakespeare was no great theologian or philosopher.

The path to wisdom he offers is a practical and pragmatic one, wherein the sum of our character is determined by adding up the small, individual actions we take in our lives—in other words, how we answer "What would Shakespeare do?" on a moment-by-moment basis. And don't worry, we've got plenty of time to get heavy later on!

So, imagine that Shakespeare is our man from the past. What would he think of our Brave New World? Tell us, Will ... what are your 21st-century turn-ons and turn-offs?

What would Shakespeare do about designer labels?

> *What's in a name? That which we call a rose*
> *By any other word would smell as sweet ...*

Juliet, *Romeo and Juliet*, II.ii.43

Do you think you have to drive a BMW to be cool? Do you have to wear dresses from Neiman-Marcus, or Guess? jeans, or Calvin Klein underwear ... just because of the name? Shakespeare says think otherwise.

My wife and I have a friend with a penchant for blister-inducing $200 Italian designer shoes. Once, at a party, she complimented my wife on the basic black pumps she was wearing. "They're so simple and elegant!" When my wife told our friend they were a comfy $19.95 knockoff brand, this woman wrinkled up her nose with a dismissive, "Oh, really?" The shoes that just moments before were "simple and elegant" had suddenly become less so—just because of the name. Shakespeare knew that it's not the label, but the essence of the thing itself that matters. And that applies to people as well as shoes.

Don't worry about labels, the Bard would say. Not only will this way of thinking keep you free of negative, prejudicial thoughts about yourself and others, but it'll allow you to buy *ten* pairs of shoes for the price of your label-obsessed friend's *one*!

What would Shakespeare do when shopping for clothes?

> *Costly thy habit as thy purse can buy,*
> *But not express'd in fancy; rich, not gaudy;*
> *For the apparel oft proclaims the man.*

Polonius, Hamlet, I.iii.70

Shakespeare lived in a well-dressed age. The Italian Renaissance cast off the utilitarian tunics and breeches of the Middle Ages and brought a panoply of slops and pantaloons, doublets and jerkins, capes, caps and bodices to a newly-prosperous Europe. But Polonius' advice to his son Laertes, who is off on a trip to France, reflects Shakespeare's practicality: your wardrobe should match your purse (the money in it, not the style and color!). Shop within your means, he says, but don't be a cheapskate, either.

Polonius suggests that if you've got some dough, and can afford a nice suit or a dress, go for it. It's likely to last longer—a practical investment that Shakespeare would definitely approve of. But beware the difference between "rich" and "gaudy"! The Bard would probably get a good laugh out of all those aesthetically-challenged boxers and football players who invariably spend their first million on gold chains, alligator boots, and big, ugly diamond rings.

And if you're not so well-heeled, Shakespeare reminds us that "the apparel oft proclaims" who we are. So even better than showing how rich you are with your clothing, show your style! I suspect the young, artistic, theatrical Bard, before he hit the big time, would have been a big fan of finding cool duds in second-hand shops.

What would Shakespeare do behind the wheel?

Celerity is never more admired
Than by the negligent.

Cleopatra, *Antony and Cleopatra*, III.vii.24

Cleopatra refers to the speed with which the Roman fleet of Caesar advances on Egypt. Having been to Rome, I can sympathize with the Queen of Nile. I, too, had the experience of a Roman army advancing fast on me—in the rear-view mirror of my rental car. Holy moly, but those modern Romans love to drive fast! It's like they all think they're Andretti or Maserati or Ferrari or Lamborghini or somebody. They roar right up your tail, slipstreaming like they're coming out of Turn 4 at Indy with the checkered flag in view and one car to beat, then ZOW they zip out into oncoming traffic and whip around the Colosseum, barely missing the phalanx of Vespas and the panini vendors and the guy dressed up like Julius Caesar who charges five bucks for you to take a photo of him with his wandering arm around your wife's hips—

But I digress.

All I'm saying is, "gentle" Will Shakespeare would urge us to show a little courtesy for other people on the road. Slow down, he'd say. Don't tailgate that ox-cart in front of you, even if it means you arrive home in Stratford ten minutes later. The point is to make sure you arrive alive, and in one piece. As Friar Laurence says in *Romeo and Juliet*, "Too swift arrives as tardy as too slow."

What would Shakespeare do about wearing sunscreen?

Thou wert better in a grave than to answer with thy uncovered body this extremity of the skies.

King Lear, III.iv.101

Shakespeare had great respect for the power of the merciless elements to mete out death. In fact, the octogenarian Lear dies the day after spending a night out under the "extremity of the skies," in a "spouting hurricanoe" of a storm. Lear had little choice in the matter. But there are lots of folks who voluntarily expose themselves to the extremities of the skies. It amazes me that some people who have enough sense to come in out of the rain often *don't* have enough sense to come in out of the sun; or at least, to wear some sunscreen.

I warned you at the outset of this chapter that some of this stuff might seem trivial. "Wear sunscreen," you say, "well, DUH! I'm not *totally* stupid." Okay, you're not, but a lot of people out there are. I see them all the time, in the parks, on the beaches, at baseball games, shirts off, hatless, skin red and peeling, blisters forming, exposing themselves to one of the most deadly—and *the* most preventable—forms of cancer. Maybe some of them are friends of yours. If so, please talk some sense into them, because preventable skin cancer is still killing people; and that, Shakespeare knows, isn't trivial at all.

What would Shakespeare do about loud-mouthed radio talk show hosts?

> *To-morrow, and to-morrow, and to-morrow,*
> *Creeps in this petty pace from day to day,*
> *To the last syllable of recorded time;*
> *And all our yesterdays have lighted fools*
> *The way to dusty death. Out, out brief candle!*
> *Life's but a walking shadow, a poor player,*
> *That struts and frets his hour upon the stage,*
> *And then is heard no more. It is a tale*
> *Told by an idiot, full of sound and fury,*
> *Signifying nothing.*

Macbeth, V.v.19

This is one of the great passages of Shakespeare, but its outlook is so bleak (things are not going at all well for Mr. Macbeth) that I feared I wouldn't be able to find a way to use it to help enlighten your life, which is the point of this book. But that bit about idiots full of sound and fury put me in mind of the world of Howard Stern wanna-be radio talk show hosts. All Shakespearean tolerance and understanding aside, I wouldn't mind lighting *those* fools the way to dusty death.

There they are every to-morrow and to-morrow and to-morrow morning at drive-time strutting and fretting their hour: "Well I tell ya what *I* think, I think (insert vicious banality here)." My wife loves 'em. She says it's great to hear how stupid all the people who call in are. I say they promote intolerance, insult our intelligence, and add stress to our already stressful morning commutes. I think Shakespeare would be on my side. My guess is he did a lot of commuting from Stratford to

London, but didn't listen to the radio much. Maybe he read a book, or boned up on his Latin or French (see page 94). Yes ... I think the Bard would listen to a lot of audiobooks and language tapes, and use the radio for listening to news or music, rather than the sound and fury of idiots.

What would Shakespeare do about the tabloids?

> *What shall I need to draw my sword, the paper*
> *Hath cut her throat already! No, 'tis slander,*
> *Whose edge is sharper than the sword, whose tongue*
> *Outvenoms all the worms of Nile, whose breath*
> *Rides on the posting winds, and doth belie*
> *All corners of the world. Kings, queens, and states,*
> *Maids, matrons, nay the secrets of the grave*
> *This viperous slander enters.*

Pisanio, *Cymbeline*, III.iv.32

There they sit, leering garishly at you from the supermarket check-out rack: sunglassed movie stars captured *in flagrante facelift*, athletes busted in late-night drug raids, politicians caught with their pants down. We know these publications are trash, right? And yet still we buy them. (Right, *you* don't, *I* don't, but *somebody's* keeping 'em in business!)

Shakespeare himself was no stranger to tabloid attacks. Early in his career, he was vilified by the lesser playwright and pamphleteer Robert Greene, who infamously called him "an upstart Crow ... [who] is in his own conceit the only Shake-scene in a country." Apparently someone complained, and the publisher of the pamphlet printed a gracious retraction ... a very rare thing in those days.

Shakespeare would tell us from first-hand experience that these venom-tongued rags do nobody any good. At best, they titillate. At worst, they destroy the lives of their victims, who are vilified with a front-page character assassination and already ruined by the time the back-page retraction is printed. So next time the checkout stand tabloid beckons, why not take a moment to remember Shakespeare's admonition against "viperous slander"?

What would Shakespeare do about "the body beautiful?"

> *In nature there's no blemish but the mind;*
> *None can be called deformed but the unkind.*
> *Virtue is beauty.*

Antonio, *Twelfth Night*, III.iv.367

The ancient Greeks believed that outward physical beauty is a mirror of internal perfection; that "beauty is virtue." For Shakespeare, the saying goes exactly the other way around: virtue is beauty. If the above quote isn't proof enough, just take a look at the cast of Greek heroes in Shakespeare's bitterly satiric *Troilus and Cressida*. They're mighty, muscular, renowned, noble ... and utterly moronic.

I think good Master Will would be mostly impressed with our society, but I think he'd be stunned that we still tend to equate physical strength and beauty with moral or intellectual merit. Elizabethans honored their great thinkers; we tend to honor vain supermodels and illiterate jocks, while our greatest poets and philosophers go unheralded. Actors and athletes enter politics and become instant sensations; a record-shattering football player/movie star can't possibly be guilty of murder; "intellectual" is a dirty word. Shakespeare would suggest that we spend less time worrying about our waistlines and pumping up our pecs, and more time improving our hearts and minds.

What would Shakespeare do if something seemed too good to be true?

> *Oftentimes, to win us to our harm*
> *The instruments of darkness tell us truths,*
> *Win us with honest trifles, to betray us*
> *In deepest consequence.*

Banquo, *Macbeth*, I.iii.123

"Free getaway vacation! (Just come see our timeshare.)" "Free phone (ten-year service contract required)." "Cigarettes make you look cool! (Very cool … in fact, cold and dead.)"

I suppose it's an encouraging commentary on human nature that we're always ready to believe that some generous soul wants to give us something for nothing—I myself have a free phone and have seen a timeshare presentation. But there are darker manifestations of the phenomenon: teens lured into hard drugs with the promise of a quick high that turns into a lifetime of addiction; lost souls lured into cults by the promise of "belonging," then cut off from their families and friends.

Shakespeare was keenly aware of the human impulse to jump at things that seem too good to be true. Reputed as he was to be gentle, honest, and upright, he wasn't one to be taken for a ride. In fact, he was known for his litigious nature, once suing a Stratford businessman for a paltry debt of 30 shillings at the same time he was buying pricey investment properties in London. The Bard looks at the world with the perpetually raised eyebrow of the writer. We'd be wise to do the same.

What would Shakespeare do about credit card debt?

Neither a borrower nor a lender be.

Polonius, *Hamlet*, III.i.75

Okay, you've heard the advice before. But do you follow it?

It's all too easy, in these days of "buy now, pay no interest 'til February 2152!" and "special 2.9% introductory rates!" to get into debt. Of course, for some things, like buying a home or a car, we must take out loans. And there's nothing wrong with loaning a friend in need a few bucks—as long as you never expect it paid back. But Shakespeare knew that these instances should be the exceptions rather than the rule. He seems to have retired to Stratford at the tender age of 44; he couldn't have done that without living thriftily.

In today's terms, that means paying off those credit cards, then paying the full balance on them every month. It means setting aside a hefty chunk of every paycheck for your retirement—as much as you can manage. It means developing and sticking to a regular plan of investing those savings.

Shakespeare was a shrewd businessman and investor, and this is definitely what he'd do about credit card debt: avoid it.

What would Shakespeare do about herbal remedies?

> *O, mickle is the powerful grace that lies*
> *In plants, herbs, stones, and their true qualities;*
> *For naught so vile that on the earth doth live*
> *But to the earth some special good doth give;*
> *Nor aught so good but, strain'd from that fair use,*
> *Revolts from true birth, stumbling on abuse.*

Friar Laurence, *Romeo and Juliet*, II.iii.15

Friar Laurence offers a moderate and sensible take on the "mickle" (mighty) power of herbal and natural remedies. Of course, in Shakespeare's day weeds and rocks were about all there was to medicine, and people died young. But have we gone too far the other direction? Are we now too dependent on the researchers at the big pharmaceutical labs, at the expense of thousands of years of herbal lore and learning?

Take the case of medical marijuana. Smoking the raw weed works better than the medically-approved pill form, but it's illegal. What are we to do? You're asking me? I say, smoking the stuff alleviates cancer patients' suffering. End of argument. Friar Laurence acknowledges the legitimate concern that its users may "stumble on abuse," but so it is with *any* drug. The only sensible answer is to legalize the weed then regulate it as any prescription drug. Maybe I'm just projecting my own opinions on those of the Immortal Bard here (not for the last time!), but I think that's exactly what Shakespeare would do with *any* such mickle medicinal herb.

What a Piece of Work is Man! (and Woman!)

"What a piece of work is man!" Hamlet says. "In action how like an angel, in apprehension how like a god." But when the melancholy Dane sadly concludes that famous speech with the miserable pronouncement, "Man delights not me," we realize that his vision of perfected humanity is an elusive one to attain.

Of course, we'll never be truly angelic or godlike. We're human, after all. We all have our tragic flaws. Hamlet's may be indecision or a tendency toward self-obsession. Ours may be jealousy, greed, dishonesty, laziness—a shocking smorgasbord of defects! But it's human nature to strive for the very mirage of perfection that we'll never attain.

What does the Bard say about problems that lie solely within ourselves? How do we overcome the less-than-angelic aspects of our character? Again, Shakespeare was a practical man, and his advice for making ourselves the best piece of work we can is no great revelation: cultivate compassion, brotherhood, humility, devotion to family and community. You know—be good, don't be bad.

Ah, if only it were that easy! Perhaps we should take it one page at a time. In this section, we look at small, incremental changes we can make to our attitudes and priorities that may help us tragically flawed humans truly become, as Hamlet says, "the beauty of the world, the paragon of animals."

What would Shakespeare do about astrology?

> *We make guilty of our disasters the sun, the moon, and the*
> *stars: as if we were villains by necessity; fools by heavenly*
> *compulsion ... drunkards, liars, and adulterers, by an*
> *enforced obedience of planetary influence ... An admirable*
> *evasion of whoremaster man, to lay his goatish disposition*
> *to the charge of a star!*
>
> Edmund, *King Lear*, I.ii.120

There are many tools we can use to improve ourselves, and get in touch with our true character. Astrology is one that's been around since well before Shakespeare's time. Is it possible that the movements of the planets affect our lives on a daily basis? Can we blame the stars for our character flaws? Sometimes it really does seem that Virgos *are* obsessively neat. That Tauruses *are* bullheaded. That Libras *are* flighty.

But I've got a theory about this. When I first read an astrology column I was probably seven or eight years old. A very impressionable age! I began to believe what the astrology columns said about me: "sensitive, moody, artistic Pisces." And the way we think about ourselves largely determines who we are. I suspect astrology columns mold us far more than the planets do.

Shakespeare is suspicious of astrology; he prefers to hold us personally responsible for our actions. But the Bard would likely approve of any tool that gets us to examine ourselves and our dreams, desires and motives. He'd have us use astrology like any tool for cultivating awareness, be it fortune-telling, psychological analysis, or even this book: use any insights we might gain to help us understand ourselves, but don't let the tool use *us;* that would deny our personal dignity, our free will, and our humanity.

What would Shakespeare do about dental hygiene?

There was never yet the philosopher
That could endure the toothache patiently.

Leonato, *Much Ado About Nothing*, V.i.35

I'm not really quoting this passage to urge you to brush after every meal, floss every day, and have a cleaning once every six months (though you should).

What's important about Leonato's tongue-in-cheek take on philosophy is this: metaphysics, for Shakespeare, takes a back seat to common sense. Ultimately, how we deal with the niggling everyday problems common to all humanity—such as toothaches—says more about our wisdom than our grasp of obtuse philosophical niceties.

Shakespeare gives an entire play over to this theme. In *Love's Labor's Lost,* the scholars of Navarre forsake food, sleep, and the company of women to pursue pure knowledge. But the more practical Berowne, a character many believe is modeled on Shakespeare himself, argues that "these are barren tasks, too hard to keep, Not to see ladies, study, fast, not sleep." Shakespeare reminds us that if we seek to understand the world, we should not turn our back on it for high-minded, self-centered, esoteric knowledge—we should embrace the world (and the ladies in it) warmly.

What would Shakespeare do if he sliced his drive deep into the rough?

> *Things without all remedy*
> *Should be without regard: what's done, is done.*

Lady Macbeth, *Macbeth*, III.ii.11

Sorry, but if I'm writing this book, you're not going to get through it without a little bit of golf philosophy. Don't worry, it applies to non-golfers, too. All good golf philosophy does.

I'm an inconsistent golfer, and it's because I have an inconsistent attitude. Some days, if I slice my first tee shot, I just laugh it off and start planning my next shot. Other days I slice the ball once and then hack my way through the rest of the round in an embarrassing spectacle of thrown clubs and ill-gotten vocabulary. Which days do you think I end up with a better score?

Shakespeare reminds us what every good golfer knows: once you've hit a bad shot, you've *got to let it go!* And life is just the same: it's about letting go of mistakes, learning from them, and moving on to the next disaster with a smile. As Lady Macbeth says, "What's done, is done." Perhaps you'll argue that slicing a ball into the rough isn't equivalent to the misdeed that plagues Macbeth: the murder of Duncan in his sleep, a deed heinous, bloody, and unnatural.

You haven't seen my golf swing.

What would Shakespeare do if he was an addict?

> *Refrain to-night,*
> *And that shall lend a kind of easiness*
> *To the next abstinence, the next more easy;*
> *For use almost can change the stamp of nature,*
> *And either master the devil, or throw him out*
> *With wondrous potency.*

Hamlet, III.iv.165

Shakespeare was ahead of his time in grasping many of the intricacies of human psychology. In this passage he presages a core precept of modern substance-abuse treatment programs: deal with your addiction one day at a time. As time goes by, the habit becomes the norm, and it gets easier, rather than more difficult, to "master the devil," i.e., to moderate or abstain.

Here Hamlet preaches daily abstinence to his mother, Gertrude, begging her to stay away from her incestuous marriage bed; but the concept applies to all addictions: drugs, booze, gambling, Nintendo, you name it.

But Shakespeare implies that the concept may also pertain to other activities besides coping with addiction. That "use," or practice, can almost change our nature. What a liberating concept, if we apply it to positive things like exercise, meditation, giving to charity, saving money. Shakespeare reminds us that if we simply start by doing it today, then do it again tomorrow and every day, one day at a time, it will eventually become an integral part of our character.

What would Shakespeare do about being honest?

> *To be honest as this world goes, is to be one man picked out of ten thousand.*

Hamlet, II.ii.178

The Bard has a bit of an odd take on honesty. Perhaps you've heard the saying, "Tell truth and shame the devil!" It's Shakespeare, true, but spoken by Hotspur, one of his least sympathetic characters. Of the foolishly generous Timon of Athens, Shakespeare says, "All men have their faults, and honesty is his." Iago, who plays on the pompous righteousness of Othello, warns us, "Take note, take note, O world,/To be direct and honest is not safe." And as for honesty in a duplicitous relationship ... well, see page 82.

Seems like Shakespeare believed that honesty was not always the best policy. And if you think about it, being brutally honest all the time would get you into some serious trouble. Telling your boss what you really think of his tie, or a friend that they seem to have put on a few pounds lately, is obviously not the way of wisdom. But there's a difference between being polite and twisting the truth to our ends to the detriment of others. I think that deep down, we know the difference between the two. And Hotspurs and Iagos aside, I think that Shakespeare would accept that it's a far nobler path to at least *try* to be the one in ten thousand.

What would Shakespeare do when deeply troubled?

> *Who alone suffers, suffers most i' th' mind,*
> *Leaving free things and happy shows behind,*
> *But then the mind much sufferance doth o'erskip,*
> *When grief hath mates, and bearing fellowship.*

Edgar, *King Lear*, III.vi.104

Despite decades of learning that our problems are best solved by communication (be it in group therapy, one-on-one counseling, or perhaps just a good chat with a trusted friend), many of us still hold our problems inside and let them fester. There's a fine line between sharing and whining, but for serious problems, it is always best to get them out in the open. Yet often those most difficult problems are the ones we hold inside.

How often we hear said of a suicide victim, "I never knew he was so troubled," or read about a serial killer, "He was such a quiet man. He kept to himself." How sad that such sickness of soul should go untended, uncared for, unministered to, just for a lack of human communication and interaction.

Shakespeare suggests that troubles are best borne with the help of others. His humanity and good fellowship remind us that if we're in trouble, we should open up to a friend; and if we have a friend in trouble, we should be a "mate" and urge them to share their grief with us, or to seek counseling. That's what gentle, good Master Will would have us do.

What would Shakespeare do in the face of rage?

> *I do oppose my patience to his fury,*
> *And am arm'd to suffer, with a quietness of spirit,*
> *The very tyranny and rage of his.*

Antonio, *Merchant of Venice*, IV.i.11

Elizabethan England was a Christian country, and Shakespeare often espouses New Testament ideals. Antonio, faced with the prospect of having a pound of his flesh cut out in payment of a debt to the loan shark Shylock, refuses to answer his rage with rage: he turns the other cheek.

The instinct to fight fire with fire is one of the most difficult human urges to overcome. Take road rage. A guy cuts me off, then honks and gives me the finger like it was my fault. My gut reaction? Sink down to his level. Give him the finger back, and scream "Aw, shaddup, ya @#$%!" Ah, but it's so much more satisfying, when I can manage it, to give him *two* fingers: a peace sign, a little wave, a smile. Not only does it make me feel better about myself, but—and here's the great unpublicized recompense of Christian meekness—it might just make the other guy feel like the @#$% he obviously is.

What would Shakespeare do about looking on the bright side?

> *There is some soul of goodness in things evil,*
> *Would men observingly distill it out.*
>
> *Henry V*, IV.i.4

For King Henry V, it's the morning of what is likely to be a disastrous battle. His troops are depleted, diseased, hungry, and outnumbered five to one by fresher and better-armed French forces. Yet Henry wakes up with the observation that at least the impending battle has gotten everyone out of bed nice and early, which, he points out, is "both healthful and good husbandry" (i.e., good time management). This king is what you'd call a glass-half-full kinda guy.

"Every cloud has a silver lining." "Always walk on the sunny side of the street." These old saws can seem as stale and flaccid as last week's lettuce. But y'know what? The alternative—being a glass-half-empty person—is just a drag.

King Harry leads his troops into battle with energy, optimism and confidence, and the result is the stunning English victory at Agincourt. Shakespeare reminds us that distilling the good out of a bad situation can be difficult, but if you succeed, you may lift yourself—and those around you—to extraordinary heights. Of course you may not succeed; but how will you know unless you try?

What would Shakespeare do when he hit bottom?

> *The worst is not*
> *So long as we can say, "This is the worst."*

Edgar, *King Lear*, IV.i.27

> *True hope is swift and flies with swallow's wings;*
> *Kings it makes gods, and meaner creatures kings.*

Richmond, *Richard III*, V.ii.23

We've all, at some time in our lives, reached a point where it seems things can't possibly get any worse. We've been dumped, we're broke, maybe jobless, even homeless ... and the worst part is, it's quite clearly our own damn fault. Well, *I've* been there, anyway. Shakespeare probably was, too. Maybe now it's your turn.

Shakespeare offers these two tidbits for solace. First, as Edgar so succinctly puts it: it can always get worse. You could be dead. Which then begs the question, why should we keep going when things get bad? Why, as Hamlet muses while contemplating suicide, should we "grunt and sweat under a weary life," when we might our "own quietus make with a bare bodkin?"

Richmond has the answer: hope. Hope is a powerful and positive force to lift us up when we're down, and can often make our wildest dreams come true. Richmond himself becomes king shortly after expressing his hopes. Maybe you can't hope to be a king these days, but you can certainly pick yourself up off the bottom and live a happy and productive life.

I hope.

What would Shakespeare do when conversing?

Brevity is the soul of wit.

Polonius, *Hamlet*, II.ii.90

Ironic that this most precise of epigrams should come from Polonius, whose verbose blather provides much of the comic relief in *Hamlet*. But then I suppose it's also ironic that Shakespeare, who wrote 37 five-act plays, 154 sonnets, and piles of poetry should also say, "Men of few words are the best men." (*Henry V,* III.ii.36)

Most windbags I know just don't get it. Take the guy who power-walks in the park where we walk our dog. Whenever we pass him, he's in the middle of a seemingly endless monologue about the most inane subjects to his walking companion (a position, by the way, that seems to have a very high turnover ratio). Everyone in that park knows him disdainfully as "Talking Guy," but he, poor man, doesn't have a clue. I'm sure he thinks he's being gregarious, outgoing, full of *joie d'vivre.* But I suspect his friends—if he has any left—wish he'd stop walking on his lower lip and let someone else get a word in edgewise for a change.

Polonius and his twaddle always gets big yuks in the theater. But just remember, "Talking Guys" are a lot more fun to watch on stage than they are to have as friends.

What would Shakespeare do about acting foolish?

> *The fool doth think he is wise, but the wise man knows*
> *himself to be a fool.*

Touchstone, *As You Like It*, V.i.30

> *O noble fool!*
> *A worthy fool! Motley's the only wear.*

Jaques, *As You Like It*, II.vii.33

Shakespeare adopted the old proverb about the wisdom of fools practically as his motto. Wise fools (or court jesters) appear in many of Shakespeare's works. With clever logic and tongue-in-cheek wordplay, they puncture the bloated pretensions of the kings and courtiers around them.

Think of the image of "The Fool" in a Tarot deck: his eyes toward heaven and smiling happily as he walks off the edge of a cliff. Yet this fool doesn't represent idiocy or ignorance, but spontaneity, freedom of spirit, innocence, the flash of divine inspiration. Like Shakespeare's "deep-contemplative" fools, his sense of wonder and faith in the universe allows him to experience life at a higher, more joyous level than worldly, narrow-minded "wise men."

Are you afraid of appearing foolish? Don't be. Shakespeare actually tells us to nurture our inner fool, to challenge accepted wisdom and dare to be different. Wear bright colors ("motley") and bells on our hats, the Bard would say; think outside the box. The capering fool in all of us brings laughter and a fresh perspective to our lives, and that, in turn, brings deeper understanding.

O noble fool, indeed!

What would Shakespeare do to keep a friend?

> *Those friends thou hast, and their adoption tried,*
> *Grapple them unto thy soul with hoops of steel.*

Polonius, Hamlet, I.iii.62

How rare is a true friend? Most of us are lucky to have one or two. And yet I know true friendships that have gone sour over the pettiest of quarrels: a forgotten thank-you note, or an insult intended in jest but taken with offense.

Hamlet and Laertes were most likely friends before the action of *Hamlet* begins, but the plots and plans of Hamlet's usurping uncle Claudius come between them, and the two vibrant young men end up killing each other in a duel. This is in stark contrast to Hamlet's friend Horatio, who stands by him even in the depths of Hamlet's torment. The final scene of the play, in which Hamlet dies in Horatio's arms, is one of the most touching in all of Shakespeare's works. When all else is lost to Hamlet—crown, family, love, life—it is Horatio who is there to pray for Hamlet's soul: "Good night, sweet prince, and flights of angels sing thee to thy rest."

Shakespeare advises us to cling to such true friends. Call them, e-mail them, buy 'em dinner every now and again, and please, try not to accidentally kill 'em in a duel.

What would Shakespeare do to keep an open mind?

> HORATIO:*O day and night, but this is wondrous strange!*
> HAMLET:*And therefore as a stranger give it welcome.*
> *There are more things in heaven and earth, Horatio,*
> *Than are dreamt of in your philosophy.*

Hamlet, II.i.160

The ghost of Hamlet's murdered father has just appeared to ask Hamlet to avenge him. Yet Hamlet's response is not one of fear, or grief, or horror, but of detached, almost eager scientific curiosity. He tells the frightened Horatio that the strangeness of the apparition should be welcomed for its own sake.

Hamlet reminds me of Jeff Goldblum's character in the *Jurassic Park* movies: an intellectual stuck in a blood 'n' guts horror flick. Hamlet, trapped in what could be a simple tale of brutal medieval vengeance, turns the story into a profound rumination on the human condition. His open, inquisitive, scientific mind makes him one of the first great modern characters, the beginning of a continuum that brings us all the way to Fox Mulder in *The X-Files*.

Shakespeare's works are filled with ghosts, fairies, sprites, apparitions, omens and supernatural wonders of all sorts. He urges us to embrace the unknown, to keep an open mind, to admit that our philosophy (i.e., science) doesn't have all the answers.

What would Shakespeare do to grieve for the dead?

> *Moderate lamentation is the right of the dead, excessive grief the enemy to the living.*

> Lafew, *All's Well That Ends Well*, I.i.55

Nothing is more difficult in this world than to let go of a loved one who has passed away. Whether it's a family member, a close friend, or perhaps a beloved pet, the hole left in our lives is always dark, cold and empty. But nature, it is said, abhors a vacuum, and that hole will fill with life once again ... if we allow it to.

Shakespeare, with his usual instinctive perception of the needs of the human psyche, suggests the healthy way to mourn in Lafew's warning to the grieving Helena: we should allow ourselves "moderate lamentation." Letting ourselves grieve for the one we've lost is the important first step in healing. But then we should get on with our lives.

To mourn excessively is to cut ourselves off from life. We might as well be mourning our own death. As Shakespeare poignantly says of Helena, "The tyranny of her sorrows takes all livelihood from her cheek." The Bard would have us remember that whoever we have lost would surely want us to move on, and live our life to the fullest, for "the time of life is short!"

What would Shakespeare do if he was stressed out?

Oh, you are sick of self-love, Malvolio, and taste
with a distempered appetite. To be generous,
guiltless and of free disposition, is to take those
things for bird-bolts that you deem cannon-bullets.

Olivia, *Twelfth Night*, I.v.90

Shakespeare crystallizes some fairly advanced psychological concepts here. Malvolio's a classic narcissist. Insecurity causes him to denigrate everyone around him in an effort to glorify himself. As a result, no one likes him, further feeding his insecurity and making him even more unpleasant. He becomes self-obsessed, unable to find joy in the world around him, unable to connect with others, increasingly trapped in the prison of his own thoughts and emotions.

Sound familiar? It's all too easy for us to get caught up in our own problems.

Shakespeare suggests the best therapy for this kind of obsession. Be generous, guiltless (i.e., don't be a finger-pointer), and of a free disposition. Or, as my wife tells me when life is getting under my skin and I'm being particularly disagreeable, "Get over your bad self!"

Gentle Will, with his recurring themes of generosity, kindness, and selflessness, reminds us that when our own concerns no longer take priority, life's daily annoyances cease to have power over us. Mountains become molehills; cannon-bullets become bird-bolts.

What would Shakespeare do if he made a big mistake?

> *No more be grieved at that which thou hast done:*
> *Roses have thorns, and silver mountains mud;*
> *Clouds and eclipses stain both moon and sun,*
> *And loathsome canker lives in sweetest bud.*
> *All men make faults.*

Sonnet #35

The real-life circumstances surrounding Shakespeare's sonnets have spawned much debate, much of which dances prudishly around what seems to yours truly to be a fairly clear-cut set of events.

1. Shakespeare writes poetry to a "wanton" young man, urging him to marry.
2. Shakespeare falls in love with said young man.
3. Young man has an affair with Shakespeare's mistress.
4. Shakespeare is mightily bummed, for obvious reasons.

That'll probably earn me a passel of letters from stuffy Shakespeare scholars, but my point is simply this: as much as he has been hurt, Shakespeare is willing to forgive his young male friend his transgression. We must remind ourselves that—however trite it sounds—to err is human, to forgive divine. We must allow faults, in each other certainly, but more importantly, in ourselves. The self-recriminations in the Sonnets suggest that Shakespeare was pretty hard on himself. But this is one thing Shakespeare would do that we needn't. Which is not to say we should revel in our faults. We can acknowledge them, try to mend them, but we can also derive comfort by remembering we're just the latest in an entire race of sinners, lechers, klutzes and bozos, stretching all the way back to Shakespeare and beyond.

Well, that comforts me, anyway.

What would Shakespeare do about poodles in sweaters?

> To gild refined gold, to paint the lily,
> To throw perfume on the violet,
> To smooth the ice, or add another hue
> Unto the rainbow, or with taper-light
> To seek the beauteous eye of heaven to garnish,
> Is wasteful and ridiculous excess.

Salisbury, King John, IV.ii.11

I'm a big fan of simplicity. This well-known—and oft-misquoted—passage indicates that Shakespeare was, too. So I hope that both he and you, gentle reader, will excuse my tirade on this subject. To wit:

The best food is simple food, simply but elegantly prepared. The greatest art is that which simply "holds the mirror up to nature." The best music is ... well, okay, I go in for pretty complex music, like Stravinsky and mid-seventies British progressive rock, *but* ... I get a nervous tic when I see a handsome dog with a lustrous coat wearing a knit sweater. I understand the appeal of SUVs, but just what exactly the hell is *up* with those HumVees, anyway? And don't get me *started* on the things women do to their bodies in the name of beauty: makeup, perfume, face-lifts, tummy tucks, and the most heinous of all the heinous examples of garnishing a beauteous thing: *breast implants*. I could go on for some time, but since I only get one page per question to rant, I'll stop now and just remind you: Shakespeare says "don't paint the lily." And Shakespeare would certainly insist that you not "gild the lily..." cuz you'd be misquoting him!

This Working-Day World

Thirty-seven plays in twenty-five years. For those of you have never written a play, take it from me: it's much harder than, say, e-mailing a joke to your friends. Then there's the poetry to write, the theater company and real estate holdings to manage, the nobles to flatter, the early retirement to plan. Shakespeare was obviously quite a successful businessman.

Of course, it's pretty easy to be successful if you sell your soul to do it. (For a whole play on that theme, look into the great work of one of Shakespeare's contemporaries: Christopher Marlowe's *Faustus*.) Just lie, cheat, steal, step on your friends and associates, and you'll probably come away from it all with a big, fat wallet.

Another path to business success is the workaholic, blow-off-your-family and die-young-of-stress-related-heart-disease route. (I think I'll pass!)

But Shakespeare's advice to us, toiling away in our cubicles and boardrooms, showrooms and shopfronts, describes how to have a successful career while still maintaining our dignity, integrity, and a healthy family and personal life. Sound too good to be true? Check it out ...

What would Shakespeare do about working 9 to 5?

> *If all the year were playing holidays,*
> *To sport would be as tedious as to work;*
> *But when they seldom come, they wished for come.*

Prince Hal, *King Henry IV Part 1*, I.ii.204

Prince Hal speaks metaphorically, suggesting that his own transformation to respectable king will be all the more stunning because of his reputation as a prodigal prince. The metaphor calls to mind a nine-to-fiver, daydreaming in a cubicle, wishing that life was one long holiday weekend.

Shakespeare suggests that we may *think* we want that, but we really don't. Just look at ancient Rome. The privileged, wealthy, Imperial citizens had so many holidays that they got bored and started feeding Christians to lions just to pass the time.

The fact is, in a normal nine-to-five job, you spend more waking hours off the clock than on. The trick is to be truly off the clock when you're off. At the end of the day, leave your work at the office. Spend your evenings with family or friends. And let your weekends be weekends: go to the beach, see a movie, take a road trip, work in the garden. And *don't* let that vacation pay go unused!

The Bard himself seemed to take time from his affairs in London to get back to the bucolic family life in Stratford; he's recorded as hoarding malt (for future batches of ale, no doubt) during a shortage in Stratford in the same year *Henry IV Part Two* and *Much Ado About Nothing* were published. Some people think this is proof that Shakespeare must have been two different people, but I think it's just a great example of how we can have a job *and* a life ... if we use our time wisely.

What would Shakespeare do to be on time?

Better three hours too soon than a minute too late.

Francis Ford, *The Merry Wives of Windsor*, II.ii.311

This is advice from the Bard I should chant like a mantra.

Are you like me? Say I'm supposed to be somewhere at 6:00 p.m. Say it's somewhere I go a lot, like my favorite Mexican cantina. Say that once, just once, on a holiday weekend Sunday morning in August when everyone else was away on vacation, it took me seven and a half minutes to get to there. Ever optimistic (see page 31) from that day forward I think, "It takes seven and a half minutes to get to El Coyote." Result? This time I'm ten minutes late, because I haven't calculated the fact that today is not a traffic-less holiday Sunday, but rush hour on Cinco de Mayo. I do that sort of thing all the time, and I'm almost always about ten minutes late.

Shakespeare reminds us that we can reduce stress in our lives, and the lives of others, by simply leaving *too much time* to get to that next meeting or appointment. So you get there a little early. It'll give you time to do a little more prep for the meeting, or do some window-shopping—or have a margarita before your other friends arrive. And aren't these all excellent things?

What would Shakespeare do to be more productive?

Great business must be wrought ere noon.

Hecate, *Macbeth*, III.v.22

Perhaps Hecate, the goddess of witchcraft and sorcery, isn't the best character to turn to for business advice. Then again, given what it takes to survive in today's business world, maybe she is.

But seriously, Shakespeare wouldn't have relied on the supernatural to get ahead in life. No—the Bard of the Ages was a champion of good, old-fashioned industriousness.

There's a saying that successful people do more before breakfast than most people do in an entire day, and there's certainly something to it. I get up reasonably early, but I'm not the type who can get out of bed at the crack of dawn on a regular basis. Yet on the rare occasions when I do, and stay focused all day, (like on the day before a long trip when I've got a million small things to take care of) I'm astounded by the amount of work I can get done. Sometimes, though, I sleep a little too late, linger over my coffee, read the paper, answer a little e-mail, then start thinking about where I'm going to have lunch. Two o'clock comes around, and I haven't done a scrap of work.

Whether it was Shakespeare's intent or not (hint: it wasn't), Hecate's witchy imprecation makes a great reminder for us to get a jump-start on our workday.

What would Shakespeare do when given new responsibilities?

> *Be not afraid of greatness. Some are born great, some achieve greatness, and some have greatness thrust upon 'em.*

Twelfth Night, II.v.143

Although this is part of an elaborate practical joke played on the servant Malvolio, cruelly convincing him that his mistress Olivia plans to marry him, it's nevertheless sage advice.

How do we respond when we find ourselves in a new and challenging situation—when greatness is thrust upon us? It can be frightening. I remember the first time I directed a major production for the theater. At the first rehearsal, I went up on stage to address the cast and crew, and there they were, thirty people whose livelihoods depended on me and my decision-making abilities over the next eight weeks, waiting for me to say and do the right things. I can only imagine what a military officer—whose soldiers' very lives depend on him or her—must feel; or, for that matter, a new parent.

We find ourselves in challenging new situations every day. Shakespeare suggests we mustn't fear them, but should see them as an adventure, an opportunity. He tells us to trust all our instincts and use all our talent and we'll do just fine.

What would Shakespeare do about being ambitious?

I charge thee, fling away ambition!
By that sin fell the angels; how can man, then,
The image of his Maker, hope to win by it?

Cardinal Wolsey, *King Henry VIII*, III.ii.440

Cardinal Wolsey should know about ambition. His head was swollen with it, and he ended up losing it. His head, that is.

Like "pride," which once had strictly negative connotations, "ambition" has come to be a respected character trait. "Young and ambitious." That describes the lawyer you want to retain to sue your insurance company. But to Shakespeare, ambition was a bad thing.

When I'm not writing books, I work in Hollywood, where I meet lots of ambitious people. Truth is, I wouldn't want to be one of 'em, because I'd have to be around myself too much. They tend to have nice salaries, nice cars, nice clothes. But they tend not to have nice friends, if they have any at all.

Shakespeare's works are filled with ambitious people—Macbeth, Julius Caesar, Mark Antony, Richard III—most of whom come to miserable, lonely ends. Gentle Will Shakespeare, who was known for his "uprightness of dealing," tells us to shun the type of ambition that turns friends, family, and co-workers into stepping stones on our climb to wealth and glory. Just work hard, respect those around you, and success will come.

What would Shakespeare do if he was promoted?

> ...'Tis a common proof,
> That lowliness is young ambition's ladder,
> Whereto the climber-upward turns his face;
> But when he once attains the upmost round,
> He then unto the ladder turns his back,
> Looks in the clouds, scorning the base degrees
> By which he did ascend.

Brutus, Julius Caesar, II.i.21

Okay, so you got that big promotion. What are you gonna do with your new power? And how will you treat your former friends—the poor, ignorant, non-upwardly-mobile yahoos who now work under you?

The reputation of newly-crowned tyrants hasn't changed from Julius Caesar's day to Shakespeare's day to today. Ladder-climbers still tend to spurn the people they used as rungs on the way up. True, there's no law that says you have to be nice to your underlings. In fact, I suspect the exact opposite rule is written somewhere in all those big black management-training notebooks.

But William "All The World's A Stage" Shakespeare knew that each of the spheres of our life is merely a microcosm of the whole. We can't just leave our morals and ethics at the front door when we go to work. And, ever-practical, the Bard would remind us that not only is treating co-workers and employees with respect just the right thing to do, it also breeds loyalty. And in today's cut-throat business world, loyalty can be a precious commodity. Just ask Julius Caesar ... who ends up stabbed and bleeding on the Capitol steps, as he implores, of his once-trusted ally, "*Et tu, Brute?*"

What would Shakespeare do about changing careers?

> *All the world's a stage,*
> *And all the men and women merely players:*
> *They have their exits and their entrances;*
> *And one man in his time plays many parts...*

Jaques, As You Like It, II.vii.139

Changing careers can be scary. But is it any scarier than the thought of remaining in a job that gives you no joy, for which you have no passion, or is not part of your dream?

Shakespeare's own life suggests the answer to this one: he played many parts. In his youth he was probably a humble worker in his father's trade. He could have taken the easy route, staying in Stratford and living a life as Will Shakespeare, tradesman, married, father of two.

It must have been a scary thing for young Will to leave his family and move to London to pursue his dream. I'll bet his wife wasn't too keen on the idea either. Yet had he not taken the plunge, who would have become the Bard of the Ages, the great playwright William Shakespeare? What a loss to the world! Later, after roles as theater owner and businessman, he returned to his hometown wealthy and successful. I suspect that Shakespeare would say, if you're in a job you don't like, and you have a dream to pursue ... what are you waiting for? Go after it!

What would Shakespeare do about changing careers AGAIN?

> *Many things, having full reference*
> *To one consent, may work contrariously:*
> *As many arrows, loosed several ways,*
> *Come to one mark.*

Canterbury, *Henry V*, I.ii.205

> *Let us follow*
> *The becking of our chance.*

Arcite, *The Two Noble Kinsmen*, I.ii.113

You may not read this advice anywhere else, but the Bard and I have something to say on the topic. You know from the previous page that it's okay to change careers once. Now that you're liberated, guess what? You can do it as often as you like! This flies in the face of traditional career counseling, which says decide what you want to be while still in diapers, then cling to it like a baby to its mother's breast, all the way to a six-figure salary, stock options, and early retirement.

Ho-hum, I say, and I think the Bard would, too. Shakespeare, it has been conjectured, followed the becking of chance into jobs as a farmer, glover, grain merchant, law-clerk, stable-boy, and schoolteacher before he even started in the theater. All these many career arrows landed on one mark: a playwright with a compassion for and understanding of people from all walks of life. Shakespeare's career path suggests that by locking into one job for a lifetime, you miss out on the dazzling variety of experiences the world has to offer.

What would Shakespeare do to relax after a hard day's work?

> *Preposterous ass, that never read so far*
> *To know the cause why music was ordained!*
> *Was it not to refresh the mind of man*
> *After his studies or his usual pain?*

Lucentio, Taming of the Shrew, III.i.9

Lucentio has disguised himself as a music teacher, the better to get into the beautiful young Bianca's pa—ah … *par*lor. Lucentio tries to draw the desirable pupil away from a rival tutor's Latin lessons by means of this argument: that music exists to rejuvenate us after intellectual or physical labor. Remember those studies that show how listening to Mozart actually increases your IQ?

Shakespeare was a music-lover. Songs and musical interludes are sprinkled liberally throughout his works. He even went so far as to suggest that, "The man that hath no music in himself, Nor is not moved with concord of sweet sounds … Is fit for treasons, stratagems and spoils … let no such man be trusted." (*Merchant of Venice*, V.i.83). For the Bard, music and the arts were the purest and noblest manifestations of the human spirit. So whether your love is Mozart, Miles, or Metallica, Bix Beiderbecke or the Beastie Boys, Shakespeare suggests that at the end of a long day, you should put down the books or the shovel, shut off the computer or vacuum cleaner, and just kick back, relax, enjoy some tunes.

Personally, I'm going to take the Bard's advice and listen to some Mozart now. I could use the IQ points.

What would Shakespeare do to get away from it all?

> Are not these woods
> More free from peril than the envious court?
> ...This our life, exempt from public haunt,
> Finds tongues in trees, books in the running brooks,
> Sermons in stones, and good in every thing.

Duke Senior, *As You Like It*, II.i.3

The duke is making the best of a bad situation: banished to the forest of Arden by his usurping brother, he offers this little ode to pastoral joy as a way of cheering up his miserable little band of "brothers in exile." Shakespeare speaks of the simple country life with an almost wistful quality, perhaps recalling his own quiet life back in Stratford.

The natural world is a tremendous source of delight and inspiration in Shakespeare's works. Images of trees and flowers, brooks and streams, wind, moon, sun and stars are ever-present. The man we remember by the pastoral nickname "The Swan of Avon" reminds us it's important for all of us to get back to nature every now and again. A day hike reminds us of the simple beauty and fragility of our planet; a night spent under the bright constellations reconnects us with the universe and provides a glimmer of our place in the scheme of things in a way that no Discovery Channel special or Stephen Hawking book can. Ah, to sit and hear those preaching stones, and read the wisdom in the running brooks.

Y'know what I'm gonna do first thing if I ever finish this book? I'm gonna go camping!

[*Publisher's Note: Jess couldn't wait, and actually finished the first draft of this book on his laptop computer—while camping next to the beautiful Kern River!*]

What would Shakespeare do when remodeling?

> *When we mean to build,*
> *We first survey the plot, then draw the model;*
> *And when we see the figure of the house,*
> *Then must we rate the cost of the erection;*
> *Which if we find outweighs ability,*
> *What do we then but draw anew the model*
> *In fewer offices, or at last desist*
> *To build at all?*

Lord Bardolph, *Henry IV Part Two*, I.iii.41

Lord Bardolph, who's carefully plotting a coup against King Henry IV, uses the building of a house as a metaphor. Most of us aren't medieval English nobility using armed insurrection to settle gripes with usurping Bolingbrokes, but Shakespeare's wisdom still works on several levels.

For one, it's good literal advice. Personally, I'm the worst of planners. I usually start a home-improvement project by going to Home Depot and buying a random bunch of wood. Then I glue and hammer pieces together until it starts to look vaguely like the thing I'm trying to build. Shakespeare recommends a more prudent approach: think ahead. Take measurements, draw up plans, determine a budget, then price out supplies and labor, and if necessary, scale down the project. As the old builders maxim goes, "measure twice, cut once."

That's good advice when planning our lives, too. Pragmatic Will would have us consider any major remodeling of our lives carefully before we take the sledgehammer to what we've already built. He would suggest having a new job lined up before quitting the old one; figure out what the long-term financial impact of that Viagra prescription would be—

Aw, come on, you didn't really think I was going to leave that "rate the cost of the erection" line alone, did you?

What would Shakespeare do about estate planning?

> *See sons, what things you are!*
> *How quickly nature falls into revolt*
> *When gold becomes her object!*

Henry IV Part Two, IV.v.64

King Henry IV is on his deathbed, watched over by his returned prodigal son, Prince Hal. The King dozes off for a minute, and wakes up to find his crown gone, taken by the Prince. Although they have a moving reconciliation in the next scene, the King's observation—that filial and sibling amity tend to fall by the wayside the moment an inheritance is at stake—is a keen one.

I hear you saying, "Oh, that would never to happen to us; our family is too close." I thought the same thing, and was shocked when a small discrepancy in our mother's will led to years of sibling legal battles.

Shakespeare himself left a very specific last will (detailed down even to the disposition of his dishes, and the famous bequest of his "second-best bed" to his wife Anne), and I'm sure he'd urge you to do the same. But Shakespeare's ultimate point is a more profound one. In the scene from *Henry IV Part Two,* the reconciliation between father and son is ultimately more important than who gets possession of the golden crown. Shakespeare would have us remember that no matter how rich the estate, no matter how valuable that heirloom jewelry or set of china, the peace and goodwill of your family is infinitely more precious.

What would Shakespeare do about diversifying his assets?

> *My ventures are not in one bottom trusted,*
> *Nor to one place; nor is my whole estate*
> *Upon the fortune of this present year.*

Antonio, *The Merchant of Venice*, I.i.41

Antonio's financial advice here is simple, age-old, and too often ignored: *don't put all your eggs in one basket.* It turns out that Antonio wasn't as well diversified as he thought he was. He ends up spread too thin, and owing a pound a flesh to the loan shark Shylock.

You think financial recommendations are out of place in a Shakespearean advice book? Remember that the Bard was a realist. "He that wants money, means and content," he says, "is without three good friends" (*As You Like It*, III.ii.24). We're all striving for contentment, and Shakespeare reminds us that our financial health (which is different from *wealth*, mind you), is just as essential to our daily happiness as our spiritual development.

William Shakespeare, investor in theater companies, real estate and the Stratford grain market, would urge you to diversify. Any sensible financial plan nowadays involves a blend of stocks, bonds, real estate and bank accounts. And it doesn't take as much to get started as you'd think. If you've got dough to blow on books about dead playwrights, you've probably got enough to invest!

Cakes and Ale

We're about halfway through this book, and so far we've adapted to twenty-first century life, dealt with some personal issues and worked on our business and financial health. I think we've earned a little break, don't you?

Too many people who get obsessed with self-improvement forget that an important part of living a well-rounded life is knowing when to stop taking everything so seriously, to let down their hair and enjoy the good things life has to offer. Eating, drinking, singing, dancing—however we acknowledge the joy of existence and find fellowship and camaraderie with our fellow revelers. Shakespeare was a man of the theater, which in itself was considered quite a debauched pastime in Elizabethan times. His plays are rich with feasts, weddings, masques and celebrations of all sorts.

In short, I believe the Immortal Bard was a major party animal.

Here we'll use Shakespeare's lust for life as a reminder to take some time out from our scurrying and carouse a little. By the way, you may find my own opinions coming out rather strongly in this section. It's one area where I am somewhat of an expert. In fact, as I write this and check my watch, I think … yes, it's happy hour!

What would Shakespeare do about booze?

MACDUFF: *What three things does drink especially provoke?*
PORTER: *Marry, sir, nose-painting, sleep, and urine. Lechery, sir, it provokes and unprovokes. It provokes the desire, but takes away the performance.*

Macbeth, II.iii.26

O thou invisible spirit of wine, if thou hast no name to be known by, let us call thee devil!

Cassio, *Othello*, II.iii.281

Though I look old, yet I am strong and lusty;
For in my youth I never did apply
Hot and rebellious liquors in my blood.

Adam, *As You Like It*, II.iii.47

Dang. It saddens me to report that Shakespeare seems genuinely not to have been fond of alcoholic beverages. Would that I could find even a shred of credible textual evidence I might twist, to project my own opinion in this case onto those of the Immortal Bard, but alas! In Shakespeare's world, booze is almost always bad news, the entertainment of thieves, villains, and rogues, a repository for poison, a prelude to murder.

Shakespeare says that to live a long and healthy life, we should avoid "rebellious liquors."

Then again, Shakespeare died at age 52.

I'm just sayin'.

What would Shakespeare do about fast food?

Unquiet meals make ill digestions.

Lady Abbess, *The Comedy of Errors*, V.i.7

Now don't get me wrong. I love a big, juicy burger with cheese sticking to the paper wrapper as much as the next guy. But we all know fast food meals are largely unhealthy, not just because of the ingredients, but because of the way we tend to eat them: on the run, in the car, at our desk while working.

The act of eating is one of the great, simple pleasures in life. Buddhist monks are not permitted to do anything but eat when they dine; it is an expression of communion with the universe, and of the unity of all things. We should let our culinary life be as balanced, and as nutritious, and as fully-appreciated, as our busy schedules allow.

That being said, it's lunchtime as I write this. I really should fill the rest of this page, but I can't help looking back longingly at that second sentence up there, about the cheeseburger....

What would Shakespeare do about eating beef?

> I am a great eater of beef, and I believe that does harm to
> my wit.
>
> Sir Andrew Aguecheek, *Twelfth Night*, I.iii.79

Now don't get me wrong. I love a juicy barbecued T-bone as much as the next beef-wit. But Sir Andrew Aguecheek is one of the great nincompoops in all of Shakespeare's canon, and he himself blames it on eating too much beef. Elizabethans believed that gorging on meat caused dull-wittedness. In fact, "beef-witted" meant "stupid" in Shakespeare's day.

Whether or not you believe that cows and chickens are somehow more "alive" than artichokes or brussels sprouts (I don't), there are some heavy issues to contend with if you're going to be a carnivore. The toll that raising animals for food exacts on our natural resources—water and grain consumption, rainforest depletion, etc. etc., is truly staggering.

Diets have changed greatly since Shakespeare's day, and mostly for the better. Sensible man that he was, I suspect the Bard would urge us to avoid becoming a beef-wit like Sir Andrew by eating a reasonably low-meat diet, heavy on fruits, veggies and whole grains. Who knows, maybe he'd even go vegetarian. But whatever he did, I know Gentle Will would respect the lifestyle choices of others, even if he disagreed with them.

What would Shakespeare do when ordering a steak?

> PETRUCHIO: *What's this? Mutton? ...*
> *'Tis burnt, and so is all the meat.*
> KATE: *The meat was well, if you were so contented.*
> PETRUCHIO: *I tell thee, Kate, 'twas burnt and dried away ...*
> *And better 'twere that both of us did fast,*
> *Than feed ... with such overroasted flesh.*
>
> *The Taming of the Shrew*, IV.ii.160

My editors think I'm talking too much about meat in this section. Maybe they're right, but Shakespeare himself was obsessed with meat. As his most famous character, *Ham*let says, "I hereafter shall think *meat*"! So ...

I'm going to ignore the fact that Petruchio is merely trying to starve Kate in order to "tame" her; ignore the fact that he's eating mutton and not, in fact, steak; ignore the fact that we have not a shred of evidence to indicate how Shakespeare ordered his steak, or indeed that he ate steak at all. I'm going to go out on a limb here and say that Shakespeare liked his steak medium rare. Cooking a perfectly tasty, tender piece of beef until it's dry and gray is a crime against humanity, the palate, and especially against the poor beast who gave its life for the greater glory of your broiler.

Before I'm off the topic of food, and while I'm still out on the limb, I'd also like to assert that Shakespeare disapproved of stewed tomatoes, but was very fond of sushi and Mexican food. Yes, I'm quite certain of that.

What would Shakespeare do about singing karaoke?

> *Heaven doth with us as we with torches do,*
> *Not light them for themselves; for if our virtues*
> *Did not go forth of us, 'twere all alike*
> *As if we had them not.*

Vincentio, Measure for Measure, I.ii.32

Bear with me on this one; it actually does come back to Shakespeare in the end.

I've got a dear friend named Laura, who, at the end of a *sake*-soaked karaoke party at a local sushi bar, was coerced into taking a turn at the microphone. Now I'd known Laura for ten years or so at this point, and never once heard her sing, so, like everyone else at the table, I cringed in expectation of that dreaded first note.

But what issued forth from those heretofore-cloistered pipes was the smokiest, sultriest rendition of Patsy Cline's "Crazy" you can imagine. Now I've known Laura for another ten years since that night, but that remains the one and only time she's let her torch-singing talent shine.

Shakespeare suggests that the heaven-sent gifts we possess are talents only if we share them with the world. Do you sing like Sinatra in the shower? Dance like Astaire with the spongemop? What are you hiding it for? Let the torch of your talent burn brightly, and light the world on fire!

What would Shakespeare do at a casino?

> *They say this town is full of cozenage*
> *As, nimble jugglers that deceive the eye,*
> *Dark-working sorcerers that change the mind,*
> *Soul-killing witches that deform the body,*
> *Disguised cheaters, prating mountebanks,*
> *And many such-like liberties of sin:*
> *If it prove so, I will be gone the sooner...*
> *I greatly fear my money is not safe.*

Antipholus of Syracuse, *The Comedy of Errors*, I.ii.97

Antipholus of Syracuse describes the ancient city of Ephesus, but it sounds to me like a travel brochure for any of the big casino towns. Ah, the glittering lights and beckoning buffets of Las Vegas ... Atlantic City ... Monte Carlo! Magicians, showgirls, 3-D interactive experiences, the umpteenth incarnation of Cirque du Soleil, and always the siren-song ching-a-ling-a-ding-ding of the casino floor.

But Shakespeare hits on the essential fact of these cities. All those pretty lights and cheap food and free drinks are a means to a single end: "cozenage." That is, parting you from your hard-earned cash.

Shakespeare tells us simply to "be gone the sooner" from these places; because the longer you stay, the more likely the odds, ever in favor of the house, will stack up against you. Me? I like to cozen 'em right back: I go and eat the buffets and the shrimp cocktails, enjoy the lights, catch a show, and get outta town without dropping so much as a dime in a slot machine.

What would Shakespeare do about carousing late at night?

> SIR TOBY: *[singing] On the twelfth day of December—*
> MALVOLIO: *... My masters, are you mad? Have you no wit, manners, nor honesty, but to gabble like tinkers at this time of night? Do ye make an alehouse of my lady's house? ... Is there no respect of place, person, nor time in you?*
> SIR TOBY: *... Dost thou think, because thou art virtuous, there shall be no cakes and ale?*
>
> *Twelfth Night*, II.iii.84

Sir Toby and his buddy Andrew Aguecheek are making an awful din late at night in Olivia's house. Her servant Malvolio comes down to quiet them down. Open and shut case, right? Shakespeare says "pipe down!"

I don't think so. Malvolio is a highly unsympathetic character: a Puritan. Puritans were ridiculed as kill-joys in the Elizabethan age, because they objected to popular revels such as the Christmastime celebration of Twelfth Night. Shakespeare's *Twelfth Night* was, in fact, probably written to be performed at Twelfth Night festivities in Queen Elizabeth's court. When Malvolio says, "do ye make an alehouse of my lady's house?" we can almost picture the actor gesturing at the Queen, who may well have been enjoying some cakes and ale herself during the holiday performance.

Toby is suggesting that Malvolio needs to get a life, and Shakespeare seems to be saying: it's a holiday—what's the problem? Get down and party!

What would Shakespeare do about chucking it all and moving to the tropics?

> ADRIAN: *The air breathes upon us here most sweetly ...*
> GONZALO: *Here is every thing advantageous to life.*
> ANTONIO: *True, save means to live.*
> SEBASTIAN: *Of that there's none, or little.*
> GONZALO: *How lush and lusty the grass looks!*

The Tempest, II.i.46

The "honest councillor" Gonzalo has the same reaction many of us have the first time we visit a tropical paradise: what am I *doing* living in a hell-hole like (fill in the name of your home town) when I could be here, swimming in the ocean every day and living on papayas and mangoes?

I'm not sayin' don't do it. I'm tempted myself sometimes. But be prepared for the facts: you're liable to get tired of mango and papaya someday; when you do there's precious little to the economy besides tourism; and ... how can I put this gently? ... not all the locals necessarily want you there.

Maybe it's best to leave these precious places relatively unspoiled, and not overrun with outsiders, yeah? Remember that in Shakespeare's works, no one ever solves their problems by running away from them. In *The Tempest*, Prospero exiles himself to a lonely island but only puts off the inevitable confrontation with his past. Shakespeare would gently suggest that we deal with our problems here and now, enjoy where we are to the fullest, and save the island getaway for a well-deserved holiday.

What would Shakespeare do if he was tired?

> *Sleep that knits up the ravell'd sleeve of care,*
> *The death of each day's life, sore labour's bath,*
> *Balm of hurt minds, great nature's second course,*
> *Chief nourisher in life's feast.*

Macbeth, II.ii.34

Spoken like a true sleep fan, Mr. Bard of the Ages!

I know people who, strange though it may seem to us normal folks, don't like to sleep. They don't like going to bed, rarely sleep well when they do, don't remember their dreams, and can't wait to get out of bed in the morning. Just in case you're one of those people:

Sleep is among life's greatest pleasures—and among its greatest mysteries, second cousin only to the Great Mystery, death. "The death of each day's life," the Bard calls it. He would have us release our cares of the day, heal our psychic wounds and refresh our bodies through sleep. Shakespeare was a lover of life, and knew its feast could best be enjoyed after a solid forty winks.

Have you had a long day? Are you getting tired of reading? Are you feeling sleepy? Is that ... a yawn? Then sleeeeepppp ... zzzzzzz.

What would Shakespeare do about being too generous?

> *Hate all, curse all, show charity to none,*
> *But let the famished flesh slide from the bone*
> *Ere thou relieve the beggar.*

Timon of Athens, IV.iii.526

No, that's not really what Shakespeare would do about giving to the needy. Of course we should give to charities, toss a panhandler a coin every now and again, and be generous with our friends—but, as the story of *Timon of Athens* suggests, we should do so within our means. Timon starts out as a great lord, a giver of feasts and parties, ever open-handed to his friends. But he goes overboard. He gives away all his land and money, falls into debt, is forsaken by his "friends," and ends up living in a cave, poverty-stricken and embittered against all charity and all humanity.

I have several friends who tend to give embarrassingly generous gifts at birthdays and during the holidays. Yet they themselves seem usually to be broke. Generosity is among humanity's noblest traits, and one that should be nurtured. The Bard simply reminds us to do so prudently. After all, many things may have changed since Timon's day ... but caves haven't gotten any more comfortable.

What would Shakespeare do if he couldn't afford to throw a big party?

Small cheer and great welcome makes a merry feast.

Balthazar, *The Comedy of Errors*, III.i.26

Good Master Will reminds us that what makes a great party is the openness and sincerity of the host, not the quality or quantity of the munchies.

Is this true? Well, let me think here. We throw a big party every Fourth of July. I get obsessed with every detail. The walkway has to be leaf-free, the house dusted as though for fingerprints at a murder scene, the hot dogs fit to serve to the Queen of England herself. My wife tries to calm me, telling me that all I have to do to throw a good party is have a good time myself and share that with our guests. It turns out the guests never notice the leaf-free walkway, the house is trashed by the second hour of the party, and despite repeated invitations, the Queen never shows.

As usual, William Shakespeare and my wife are both right. All you need to throw a great party is the desire to do so, and an open heart with which to welcome your guests.

What would Shakespeare do to honor Christmas?

> *Some say that ever 'gainst that season comes*
> *Wherein our Savior's birth is celebrated,*
> *This bird of dawning singeth all night long,*
> *And then, they say, no spirit dare stir abroad,*
> *The nights are wholesome, then no planets strike,*
> *No fairy takes, nor witch hath power to charm:*
> *So hallowed and so gracious is that time.*

Marcellus, *Hamlet*, I.i.157

This little ode to the sanctity of Christmas may seem a little out of place in the midst of the brooding opening scenes of *Hamlet*, but it brings light to a dark moment. Marcellus explains how the crowing of a rooster, which has just frightened away the ghost of Hamlet's father, traditionally rings in the sacred holiday season.

It's easy to be cynical about Christmas, its commercialization and sentimentality, its dreaded family reunions and boat-anchor fruitcakes.

But celebrating and giving thanks during the long winter months is a component of all major religions, past and present. It's an impulse as old as humanity itself, and has spawned a long tradition of literature (Dickens' *A Christmas Carol*, Dylan Thomas' *A Child's Christmas in Wales*, and Dr. Seuss' *How the Grinch Stole Christmas*, to name my three personal favorites) that urges us to look beyond crassness in the Christmas season to its true meaning: thankfulness, brotherhood, sisterhood, compassion, peace. These, Shakespeare suggests, are things that we can and should celebrate without cynicism, no matter what our religion ... and no matter what the time of year.

Love's Labor's Won

We can all use some advice when it comes to love. Even during the course of my writing this book, I've had friends take me aside and say, "So what would Shakespeare do about getting someone you like to like you back?"

For the lovers in Shakespeare's works, finding true love is an uphill climb. At best, it usually takes five acts of convoluted farce to get to the happy wedding day. And in the tragedies ... well, lovers don't do well at all in the tragedies.

All the evidence suggests that Shakespeare himself didn't have a particularly easy love life, either. Judging by the tortured lust and self-doubt revealed in his Sonnets, with their ongoing, steamy soap opera involving Shakespeare, a young nobleman, a rival poet and the mysterious Dark Lady, Shakespeare seems to have had plenty of experience in the deep, dark trenches of love.

Perhaps that's why he speaks with such rare passion and pathos about love's ups and downs. He himself must have learned the patience, honesty and compromise it takes to maintain a relationship. There are few explorations of love more rich and varied than the works of William Shakespeare. Here we can find a mountain of advice that just may make our own five-act farce of a love life a bit easier to bear.

What would Shakespeare do to tell the difference between love and lust?

> Love comforteth like sunshine after rain,
> But Lust's effect is tempest after sun;
> Love's gentle spring doth always fresh remain;
> Lust's winter comes ere summer half be done;
> Love surfeits not, Lust like a glutton dies;
> Love is all truth, Lust full of forged lies.
>
> *Venus and Adonis*, 799

So there's someone who's on your mind, and you want to know: is it love or lust? El Bardo Grande gives us a pretty good checklist. Let's just run it down.

When thinking of this person, do you feel comforted? Sounds like love. Or is your mind a raging storm? Sounds like lust. Are encounters with this person "always fresh," or do you tend to get weary of them between bouts of passion? If the former, love; the latter, lust. Lust, the Bard suggests, is gluttonous—you tend to be jealous and controlling. But love isn't greedy about the other person's time—you delight in being together but leave room for being apart. Are you "all truth" with this person? Love. Or do you make up lies to try to win them over? Lust.

It comes down to this: love is always about the other person; lust is always about you. So, do you want to be there for the other person? Or do you just want them to be there for you? If you can answer that question honestly, you'll know whether it's love or lust.

What would Shakespeare do about falling "madly" in love?

> ROMEO: *Love-devouring death do what he dare,*
> *It is enough I may but call her mine.*
> FRIAR: *These violent delights have violent ends,*
> *And in their triumph die, like fire and powder,*
> *Which as they kiss consume ...*
> *Therefore love moderately: long love doth so.*
>
> *Romeo and Juliet*, II.vi.7

For Shakespeare, love wasn't all a bed of roses by another name. It was just as likely to be a subject for tragedy as for comedy. The blind passions of Romeo and Juliet, Antony and Cleopatra, and Othello and Desdemona all lead to exactly the "violent ends" that Friar Laurence fears.

Like Romeo, we tend to romanticize this type of mad passion and think of it as "true love." We may sacrifice our careers, our dignity, even our lives in an obsessive quest for the object of our desire. But Friar Laurence urges a more "moderate" type of love (prime examples of which are to be found not in Shakespeare's tragedies, but in his comedies). If you're looking for Master William's model couple, forget Romeo and Juliet and check out the lovers in *Much Ado About Nothing* or *The Taming of the Shrew.* They begin with outright animosity, then move into an elaborate courtship dance where the couples carefully explore each other's foibles before coming to that point of compromise and equilibrium where love may truly flourish. This, Shakespeare suggests, is the kind of love that lasts. The kind where you end up married, not murdered.

What would Shakespeare do about unrequited love?

> *Say that she rail; why then I'll tell her plain*
> *She sings as sweetly as a nightingale:*
> *Say that she frown, I'll say she looks as clear*
> *As morning roses newly wash'd with dew:*
> *If she do bid me pack, I'll give her thanks,*
> *As though she bid me stay by her a week.*

Petruchio, *The Taming of the Shrew*, II.i.170

Petruchio intends to win over the notoriously hostile Kate by lavishing kindness upon her. Good plan. It's a technique that can help you get what you're after in all sorts of circumstances. Amiability is so rare these days that people tend to get flustered if you're nice to them. Try it when dealing with your bank, credit card company or local Motor Vehicles Department. (Actually, I take that last one back. The DMV is a hopeless case.)

And killing 'em with kindness, à la Petruchio, is a particularly potent way to woo a reluctant heartthrob. I oughta know, it was used on me to great effect by a woman once. No matter how mean I was to her, she just kept smiling, never gave up—always giving me little gifts, surprising me with unannounced visits—in fact, her behavior bordered on harassment. I probably could have gotten a restraining order. Whenever I bring that up to her, now that we're happily married, she tells me: "Hey, it's not stalking if you care."

But being nice isn't just a ploy for getting what you want in life. Shakespeare said "beauty lives with kindness." He believed we can actually make the world a more beautiful place simply by being civil to each other.

What would Shakespeare do (or not do) on a first date?

> JULIET: *Although I joy in thee,*
> *I have no joy of this contract tonight;*
> *It is too rash, too unadvised, too sudden;*
> *Too like the lightning which doth cease to be*
> *Ere one can say it lightens. Sweet, good night!*
> ROMEO: ... *O, wilt thou leave me so unsatisfied?*
>
> *Romeo and Juliet*, II.ii.117

Juliet and Romeo have fallen for each other at first sight, and although they've just met, Romeo leaves Juliet's bedroom balcony only under duress. If Shakespeare shows some sympathy with the raging of Romeo's youthful hormones—the sexual innuendo of "wilt thou leave me so unsatisfied?" is no accident—Juliet's hesitancy suggests that they're moving too fast for a first date. The tragic ending of the play proves Juliet right: their sudden passion is indeed rash and unadvised.

Romeo and Juliet is a great story, but a terrible model for how to conduct a relationship. In real life, they would have done well to "say good night" indeed after their date, take it slow, think about the possible consequences of their actions, and proceed in a measured way toward developing a mature relationship. The Bard would certainly counsel us to do the same.

Oh, and Shakespeare would also remind us to use condoms. I'm sure Willy would be literally tickled pink by the variety and sensitivity of today's prophylactics.

What would Shakespeare do to woo a woman?

> *Flatter and praise, commend, extol their graces ...*
> *That man that hath a tongue, I say, is no man,*
> *If with his tongue he cannot win a woman.*

Valentine, The Two Gentlemen of Verona, III.i.102

Call it old-fashioned, but most women love to hear men speak their love-thoughts out loud. So go ahead! The woman's beautiful, right? Tell her so! She'll love to hear it. And, ladies, that goes for men too. Men aren't nearly as sensitive to subtle signals as you are. Man or woman, young or old, rich or poor, Shakespeare advises us to tell 'em how you feel. The Bard clearly insinuates that language is the best tool for romance.

But that's not the only insinuation in the passage. He suggests another tool for love. Shakespeare, you know, was one bawdy dude. When it came to sex he knew all about the birds and the bees, and every species in between. He also seems to have had a fairly astute sense of what gives a woman pleasure.

Believe me, when he says a man is no man if he can't win a woman with his tongue, he's not just talkin' about talkin', if you catch my drift.

And yes, that goes for women's tongues, too!

What would Shakespeare do to woo a woman if he was tongue-tied?

> *Win her with gifts, if she respect not words:*
> *Dumb jewels often in their silent kind*
> *More than quick words do move a woman's mind.*

Valentine, *The Two Gentlemen of Verona*, III.i.89

This advice from the Bard is four hundred years old, and some of my female friends wish that the custom of "buying a woman with a rock" (as they put it) had been put to bed long before that.

But I think they're the minority.

The exchange of rings and baubles as tokens of love and friendship has a long and rich history, and regardless of the tradition's roots in a paternalistic, women-are-property society, there's still nothing like a jewel for expressing your affection. That's why even today, asking someone to marry you without producing a ring (in my very humble experience) tends to be taken as some kind of joke.

But again, this advice isn't just for men. In his will, Shakespeare left money to his closest friends "to purchase memorial rings." We *all* love receiving gifts. Sure, my wife knew I really wanted to marry her when I gave her the ring. But I also knew she really cared for me when she bought me tickets to a hockey game ... and actually went with me ... *and* cheered for my team! Now *that's* the way to woo a lover!

What would Shakespeare do to get a man ... uh ... if he was a woman, that is?

> Can it be
> That modesty may more betray our sense
> Than woman's lightness?...
> Never could the strumpet,
> With all her double vigor, art and nature,
> Once stir my temper; but this virtuous maid
> Subdues me quite.
>
> Angelo, *Measure for Measure*, II.ii.167

Here Angelo confronts an age-old question: do men like their women modest and mild, or wet and wild? You want the straight dope from the Bard on this one? Okay, here it comes ...

It depends on the man.

Angelo finds himself surprised at the degree to which Isabella's modesty turns him on, where a painted prostitute never could. But other Shakespearean characters like their women bolder and more sensuous —just think of Marc Antony and Cleopatra. Shakespeare had a sharp eye for such individual quirks, and how those quirks work together to create romance. The Bard would scoff at all those magazines that claim to know the ten "guaranteed" turn-ons, or books that tell us that all men and all women are from different planets. He knew that men and women fit together like jigsaw puzzles, not Velcro. We are all gloriously unique individuals, and different things stir our souls and our libidos.

What Angelo is really responding to is Isabella's strength of character, and this hints at the Bard's best advice for finding a mate: be yourself and be comfortable with who you are—nothing is more attractive than genuine confidence.

What would Shakespeare do (that you probably shouldn't) about gender equality?

> ... Thy husband is thy lord, thy life, thy keeper,
> Thy head, thy sovereign; one that cares for thee ...
> Whilst thou li'st warm at home, secure and safe.
> ... Place your hands below your husband's foot;
> In token of which duty, if he please,
> My hand is ready, may it do him ease.

Katharine, *The Taming of the Shrew*, V.ii.146

Some scholars suggest that Katharine's admonition—that women should literally let their lords and masters walk all over them—was ironic. Sorry. Shakespeare simply echoes the Elizabethan ideal for a proper woman: loving, obedient, subservient. I can hear the drumbeat of a chauvinist army grunting, "Yes! Yes! Yes!" at this proclamation of male superiority, but keep in mind: Shakespeare wrote these words 400 years ago. At the time, people also believed in the divine right of kings, public dismemberment of convicts, and bathing once a year. We over here in the human race like to think we've grown a little, intellectually, morally and hygienically, in four centuries.

I would urge you, dear reader, to ignore Shakespeare's dated take on the subject. Instead, look at the example of someone who was proving the Bard's assessment of proper gender relations flawed even as he penned it. Shakespeare's own lord, king, governor, and sovereign at the time was Queen Elizabeth I—a single woman, and perhaps the most successful monarch in English history.

Hey, when are we gonna get a woman U.S. President, anyway?

What would Shakespeare do if he had a mistress? Would he tell his wife?

> *If you did wed my sister for her wealth,*
> *Then for her wealth's sake use her with more kindness:*
> *Or if you like elsewhere, do it by stealth ...*
> *Be secret-false: what need she be acquainted?*
> *... Ill deeds is doubled with an evil word.*

Luciana, *The Comedy of Errors*, III.ii.10

This is surely one of the most difficult ethical questions there is. Shakespeare himself was almost certainly an adulterer, with his wife in Stratford and his Dark Lady in London. How did he deal with it? Luciana's advice to Antipholus of Syracuse, whom she believes is cheating on her sister, is to keep it secret. Luciana is a highly sympathetic character, the voice of reason in this play. Is Luciana's advice merely Shakespeare, justifying his own actions to himself? Or would the Bard really advise us to be "secret-false" about our peccadilloes?

I believe Shakespeare, ever compassionate and yet ever practical, would have us at the very least carefully consider our motives before we spill the beans. If you tell your spouse about an indiscretion, are you clearing the air to allow for an honest re-assessment of your relationship? Or are you trying to make yourself feel better? Or are you actually trying to hurt your spouse? Or is it just a quick and dirty way of ending the relationship?

The only easy answer here is suggested by Luciana at the outset: "treat her with more kindness"—a good idea in any circumstance. If you're married, honor your vows; don't get yourself into a position where you even have to *answer* this question. Maybe that's what Shakespeare would do—if he could do it all over again.

What would Shakespeare do about a relationship in trouble?

> LYSANDER: *For aught that I could ever read,*
> *Could ever hear by tale or history,*
> *The course of true love never did run smooth ...*
> HERMIA: *If then true lovers have been ever cross'd ...*
> *Then let us teach our trial patience,*
> *Because it is a customary cross,*
> *As due to love as thoughts and dreams and sighs,*
> *Wishes and tears.*
>
> *A Midsummer Night's Dream*, I.i.32

In the world of Shakespeare's comedies, it takes perseverance—through five acts of misunderstandings, mistaken identities, mislaid messages, mistrustful parents, and a whole lotta cross-dressing—to reach a happy ending.

But many of us don't have the patience for five acts worth of conflict in our love lives. We want the happy ending to come in Act One. We expect too much from love, and then give up on it too easily. Jerry's character on *Seinfeld* is the poster child for modern love: a different hot date every week, each rejected for a different flaw—too tall, too short, too medium-height ...

Shakespeare urges us to realize that strong relationships develop not just from instant attraction, from moon-eyed "dreams and sighs," but by toiling together through the adversity that tests every relationship. In real life, turning your love life to tragedy is easy. But to write a happy ending to your own love story takes understanding, forgiveness, compromise and a whole lot of hard work.

What would Shakespeare do if he got dumped?

> BENVOLIO: *Be ruled by me: forget to think of her.*
> ROMEO: *O teach me how I should forget to think!*
> BENVOLIO: *By giving liberty unto thine eyes:*
> *Examine other beauties.*

Romeo and Juliet, I.ii.225

In the first scene of *Romeo and Juliet*, Romeo is miserable with lovesickness—not for Juliet, but for another Italian beauty named Rosaline, who rejects him in favor of a *life of chastity*. Owch, that's *gotta* hurt!

Getting over a relationship that's over is tough. Supposedly it takes six months for every year the relationship's lasted. But if you find yourself obsessed with your ex for longer than that, it's time to take control, and Benvolio suggests the right process to Romeo: simply make the choice to get over it, he says. No matter how hard it is, *don't let yourself think about 'em*! Make yourself go to a party, a bar, whatever, and look at the other appetizers on the menu of love. It may be difficult or impossible at first, but after awhile you can actually train yourself to open up and be emotionally ready for the main course: a new partner.

Just look at Romeo. He reluctantly takes Benvolio's advice, goes to the big party at Signior Capulet's place, is immediately stricken with the ha-cha-chas for Juliet and forgets Rosaline ever existed. Of course, the whole Juliet thing doesn't turn out too well for him either. Romeo really needs to work on his relationship skills. Maybe I'll send him a copy of this book.

What would Shakespeare do about STDs?

The gods are just, and of our pleasant vices make
instruments to plague us.

Edgar, *King Lear*, V.iii.172

Sexually transmitted diseases: I'd like to be able to say that Shakespeare, in his wisdom, avoided them like the plague. But in Shakespeare's London, STDs were as rampant as the plague itself. In fact, there is some speculation that Shakespeare himself had syphilis. The dialogue of his many prostitute and pimp characters—and the gentlemen who visit them—is rife with puns about the disease's symptoms (which include —ahem—premature baldness).

Shakespeare is no Puritan, and he never says we shouldn't have any "pleasant vices." We're human, after all, and human frailties are a playwright's bread and butter! But he suggests that earthy vices bring earthy consequences, and we must be prepared to accept the gods' retribution.

Whether it's a hangover in exchange for a night of boozing it up or STDs in exchange for unprotected sex, Shakespeare reminds us we reap what we sow.

What would Shakespeare do about gay marriage?

> Let me not to the marriage of true minds
> Admit impediments. Love is not love
> Which alters when it alterations finds
> Nor bends with the remover to remove ...
> Love's not Time's fool, though rosy lips and cheeks
> Within his bending sickle's compass come;
> Love alters not with his brief hours and weeks,
> But bears it out, even to the edge of doom.

Sonnet #116

Okay, maybe Shakespeare wasn't talking specifically about gay marriage. But maybe he was. The literary London of Queen Elizabeth's day was a progressive scene. Check out the portrait of Shakespeare on the cover of this book. Note the earring. Note the sensitive eyes. He's a handsome man, don'tcha think? And take another look at Shakespeare's early sonnets. Among many other tender endearments, the famous "Shall I compare thee to a summer's day? Thou art more lovely, and more temperate" (Sonnet #18), is addressed not to a beautiful woman, but to a young nobleman.

Shakespeare's sexual orientation aside, Sonnet #116 is an eloquent treatise on the power of love. For the poet, love transcends time, separation, changing circumstances ... may it not transcend gender as well?

There is a shortage of love and commitment in this world. Maybe I'm wrong, but I think Shakespeare, a champion of compassion and tolerance, would urge us to support love and commitment, and not admit impediments to marriage between *any* two true minds.

What would Shakespeare do if he was truly, deeply in love?

> *What is love? 'Tis not hereafter;*
> *Present mirth hath present laughter;*
> *What's to come is still unsure.*
> *In delay there lies no plenty,*
> *Then come kiss me, sweet, and twenty;*
> *Youth's a stuff will not endure.*

Twelfth Night, II.iii.47

So, have you built a love strong and true? Neither lust nor a blind, unrequited torment, but a love "as sweet and musical as bright Apollo's lute"? Then, Shakespeare says, live it every moment, every day, for all it's worth, because love is, as Hermia puts it in *A Midsummer Night's Dream*, "swift as a shadow, short as any dream, brief as the lightning." For Shakespeare, a deep, true love was a precious, fragile, fleeting thing, to be enjoyed not "hereafter," but right now. He tells those of us who are lucky enough to be in love to revel in it. Enjoy the delicious feeling while it lasts, for perhaps even the love that now seems so secure will, like our youth, someday fade.

Bittersweet, isn't it, that love is so frail? But for the Sweet Swan of Avon, its very fragility is what makes love so alluring; he knew that living in constant awareness of its transience can make our experience of love that much more powerful. Shakespeare urges us not to take our love for granted, but laugh, kiss, kiss more, and kiss twenty times—quick, before it's too late!

Noble Youth,
Tender Youth,
Bloody Youth

Noble, tender, bloody—these are just three of the dozens of epithets a simple search for "youth" yields on my favorite Shakespeare website. Burning, riotous, humorous, giddy, unstaid, vain, unhappy, wilful, blessed … Shakespeare rightly saw youth as the most varied and challenging time of our lives. The pangs of first love, the awakenings of sexual awareness, the struggle to create an identity and maintain self-respect, all while having to go to school and beginning to think about a career … those "best years of your life" can get pretty crazy.

Let's face it, it hasn't gotten any easier in the past 400 years. But for Shakespeare, youth is the furnace in which our character is forged. The choices we make in our youth—and especially the mistakes and lapses of judgment, and what we learn from them—determine what kind of adults we will become.

Forging the kind of adults the Bard would have us be—compassionate, tolerant, gentle—requires an upbringing based on understanding, respect and love. I hope the bits of the Bard's wisdom offered in the next few pages will make your youth—or the youth of someone near and dear to you—noble and tender, rather than bloody.

What would Shakespeare do about "kids today"?

> *I would there were no age between ten and three-and-twenty ... for there is nothing in the between but getting wenches with child, wronging the ancientry, stealing, fighting.*

Shepherd, The Winter's Tale, III.iii.59

Today, restless kids rove in gangs and kill each other in the mean city streets—just like in *Romeo and Juliet*. Psychologically abused sons murder their stepfathers—just like in *Hamlet*. Ungrateful offspring disrespect and abuse their elderly parents—just like in *King Lear*.

According to some distraught talk-show moms, "kids today" are some sort of alien bodysnatching brood, violent, rash, incomprehensible, and nothing like the angelic paragons of virtue that *we* were as kids.

Hogwash. As the shepherd's lament suggests, "Kids today" have always been "kids today."

But Shakespeare's plays also suggest ways to raise children into responsible, civil adults. *Romeo and Juliet* hints at the dangers of leaving child-rearing to a nurse or nanny; the tortured Hamlet is the by-product of a mother who, with her o'er-hasty re-marriage, thought little about the feelings of her son; *King Lear* chronicles the regrets of a man who pronounces a rash judgment on his favorite child. We should consider these examples and stay involved in our kids' growth and learning, be sensitive to their concerns, be patient, and above all not be too selfish. Involvement, understanding, patience: Shakespeare suggests that these are the prescription for keeping children from tragic ends.

What would Shakespeare do about disciplining a child?

> *Now, as fond fathers,*
> *Having bound up the threatening twigs of birch,*
> *Only to stick it in their children's sight*
> *For terror, not to use, in time the rod*
> *Becomes more mock'd than fear'd.*

Duke Vincentio, *Measure for Measure,* I.iii.23

Shakespeare's *Measure for Measure,* as the title suggests, explores themes of crime and punishment, of how we measure the damage inflicted on society by a crime and then measure out appropriate justice.

Here Shakespeare literally brings the issue home to the domestic level, by suggesting what modern child development specialists now know: children should be taught the boundaries of acceptable behavior, understand the penalties for transgressing those boundaries, and *see those penalties fairly imposed* when they cross the line.

Now I'm no fan of corporal punishment, and I personally hope you never strike a child. I always get a little queasy when I see some stressed-out adult in a supermarket swat a kid because he's had the temerity to ask for a comic book or a candy bar. But whether we use "time outs" or "twigs of birch" to discipline a child, Shakespeare reminds us to let *consistency* be our guiding principle. If we threaten a child with a grounding when she comes in after curfew, but then let her slide for no good reason, we—and the punishment—have lost respect and authority, and the child gains only an awkward sense that, for better or for worse, the world can't be trusted.

What would Shakespeare do to educate his children?

> PROSPERO: ... *Here*
> *have I, thy schoolmaster, made thee more profit*
> *Than other princess' can, that have more time*
> *For vainer hours, and tutors not so careful.*
> MIRANDA: *Heavens thank you for't!*
>
> *The Tempest,* I.ii.171

Many critics think that Prospero is an alter ego for Shakespeare. He's also an extreme example of a parent who takes pains to be involved in the education of a child. Exiled on a desert island with nothing but his daughter and his books, he's devoted himself wholeheartedly to Miranda's education; and she is, as her name implies, a wonder.

The historical William Shakespeare took the opposite approach from his alter ego. Although his eldest daughter, Susanna, was reputedly quite urbane, a chip off the old block, his younger daughter Judith signed her name with an "X." This has caused some puzzlement among scholars, but to me the explanation seems common enough: Shakespeare's career took precious time away from his kids. "I'm sorry, Anne," we can hear the Immortal Bard saying, "but the first draft of *Lear* is due next week and I'm on the morning coach to London for the dress rehearsal of *Othello*—I don't have *time* to help Judith with her ABCs."

We should err on the side of Prospero's approach. You don't need to strand yourself on a desert island for 15 years of non-stop tutelage, but Shakespeare—Judith, that is—would tell you there's no substitute for learning one-on-one with Mom or Dad.

What would Shakespeare do when dealing with his parents?

> *How sharper than a serpent's tooth it is*
> *To have a thankless child!*

King Lear, I.iv.288

What happens when children don't treat their parents with respect? Shakespeare devotes an entire play, *King Lear*, to an exploration of filial ingratitude. Lear abdicates his throne and divides his kingdom between his two eldest daughters. They treat him like dirt in return, and what happens? Everyone ends up tragically, epically dead.

King Lear is one long reminder to all of us "of woman born" to be cool to our parents. I hear some of you saying, "You've obviously never met my folks." True, just like cranky old Lear himself, our parents can seem overprotective, unsympathetic, demanding. But if they've treated us reasonably well, or at least tried to, they deserve our honor.

But Shakespeare also knew that filial gratitude is a two-way street. Lear's troubles begin when he mistreats his youngest daughter, unjustly banishing and disinheriting her. Obviously, we can't abuse our children and then expect them to honor us in our old age. The story of Lear tells us that the best way for parents to ensure their children will be a comfort in their old age, and not a serpent's tooth, is to treat them with respect.

What would Shakespeare do about learning a language?

What is "pourquoi?" To do, or not do? I would I had bestowed that time in the tongues that I have in fencing, dancing, and bear-baiting. O, had I but followed the arts!

Sir Andrew Aguecheek, *Twelfth Night*, I.iii.91

I was recently on a research trip in Italy and Greece, and discovered that nearly everyone there speaks some English. Many speak one or two other languages as well—German, French, Spanish—in addition to their native tongue. In Shakespeare's day, even the state-run grammar schools taught classical languages. The Bard wrote an entire scene (in *Henry V*) in French. And yet Shakespeare's friendly rival Ben Jonson crowed that Shakespeare knew "little Latin and less Greek." Jeez, how many friends do you have who know *any* Latin or Greek? What a sign of the vibrant culture and learning of Elizabethan England!

I think Shakespeare would be shocked to see that in English-speaking countries today, so few people are bilingual. Sure, math, business, and science are important, and playing basketball or football is fun (bear-baiting has, thankfully, gone out of vogue). But someday—maybe when that sexy Spaniard is looking at you with come-hither eyes—you'll wish you knew what "*Hola, mi amor! Te amo! Te adoro!*" meant. So, yo! Take a cue from Mr. Ague: learn a language—or two!

What would Shakespeare do when declaring a major?

> *The mathematics, and the metaphysics,*
> *Fall to them as you find your stomach serves you:*
> *No profit grows where there is no pleasure ta'en.*
> *In brief, sir, study what you most affect.*

Tranio, *The Taming of the Shrew*, I.i.37

I'm going to get in trouble here with a whole passel of education reformers who chant the mantra, "more math and science, more math and science, more math and science." Science is great, and math is the language spoken by the universe. But here Shakespeare gives sage advice: study what you love most, be it math, philosophy or basket weaving.

Too many parents force their children into a life of unfulfilled misery by insisting they become scientists or lawyers or doctors, without considering where the child's true passion lies.

I'm fortunate. Though I was told by countless wizened elders to study algebra "because I'd use it someday," and by countless others not to study Shakespeare in college because I'd "never use an English degree," my parents (bless 'em!) told me to study whatever I wished. Well, here I am making a decent living writing about Shakespeare—and still waiting for the day I have to solve a quadratic equation in real life.

Shakespeare, like all great thinkers, simply urges us to follow our dreams.

What would Shakespeare do about "hitting the books?"

> *Study is like the heaven's glorious sun*
> *That will not be deep-search'd with saucy looks*
> *Small have continual plodders ever won*
> *Save base authority from others' books.*
> *These earthly godfathers of heaven's lights*
> *That give a name to every fixed star*
> *Have no more profit of their shining nights*
> *Than those that walk and wot not what they are.*

Berowne, *Love's Labor's Lost*, I.i.84

Berowne plays the devil's advocate in a debate about the value of book-learning. He implies that "continual plodders" (those who spend their lives with their noses in books) learn nothing except the rehashed opinions of other plodders; that if you spend your nights at a desk poring over a star chart, giving names to stars, you'll enjoy them no more than if you just go for nighttime walk and appreciate their beauty.

Berowne knows he's overstating the case, as does Shakespeare. Of course study is valuable. But book-learning without life experience makes one shallow, uninteresting—in a word, a geek. Shakespeare's life prior to his arrival in London helped make him a greater playwright, more in tune with the wide breadth of humanity, than any of the more learned, university-educated writers of his day. Shakespeare urges us not merely to read about life, but to live it. This is how great thinkers, inventors, actors, artists—and playwrights—are made.

What would Shakespeare do to expand his horizons?

> *Home-keeping youth have ever homely wits.*
> *... I rather would entreat thy company,*
> *To see the wonders of the world abroad,*
> *Than (living dully sluggardized at home)*
> *Wear out thy youth with shapeless idleness.*

Valentine, *The Two Gentlemen of Verona*, I.i.2

The settings of Shakespeare's plays read like the itinerary of a college student's whirlwind European tour: Paris, Vienna, Venice, Florence, Verona, Milan, Rome, Athens. In fact, his obvious fascination with the continent of Europe has spawned much conjecture as to whether he spent time there. Some is dubious ("Shakespeare had to be a noble, because only nobles could travel to the continent"), some intriguing (Shakespeare traveled to the continent as a young man, perhaps as a player in a touring theater company), some comic ("Shakespeare was actually Italian!").

But whether or not Shakespeare ever barnstormed through Europe, his plays clearly revel in the "wonders of the world." Many of the comedies begin with a sea voyage or a fresh-faced youngster arriving in an unfamiliar place in search of love, wealth or adventure.

Shakespeare knew that travel enriches us. Puffed-up self-satisfaction with our own culture gets punctured by the needle of new attitudes; we get a healthy dose of seeing ourselves through others' eyes. We return wiser, more tolerant, more worldly, and ... well, just plain *cooler*. "So what're you waiting for?" Shakespeare would ask. "Start saving now for those airline tickets!"

What would Shakespeare do if he was stranded in a strange country?

> *What's to do?*
> *Shall we go see the relics of this town?...*
> *I pray you, let us satisfy our eyes*
> *With the memorials and things of fame*
> *That do renown this city.*

Sebastian, Twelfth Night, III.iii.18

Sebastian is definitely making the best of a bad situation. He's just nearly drowned in a shipwreck which he believes has killed his beloved twin sister; he's been cast up on the shores of a strange foreign land, and decides to answer his cruel fate by ... doing a little *sightseeing?!*

Brilliant dramatist though he was, Shakespeare's character motivations sometimes got a little sloppy. But Sebastian's curiosity about the relics and antiquities to be found in a strange city is an urge I can relate to. Whenever my wife and I are traveling, I'm the one with the dog-eared guidebook, plotting out a grueling course of churches, museums, fountains and plazas that would leave mere sightseeing amateurs with bleeding stumps where their feet used to be.

But I find all the pavement pounding worthwhile, and the sights exhilarating. My guess is that the Bard, too, traveled to the great cities of Europe, and that he also found them inspiring. Exploring the past of a city connects us with our human heritage; it gives us a perspective on our place in the inexorable flow of history. Incidentally ... have you checked out all the "memorials and things of fame" in your *own* town?

What would Shakespeare do when he returned home after traveling?

> Farewell, Monsieur Traveler. Look you lisp and wear
> strange suits, disable all the benefits of your own country,
> be out of love with your nativity, and almost chide God for
> making you that countenance you are; or I will scarce
> believe you have swam in a gondola.

Rosalind, As You Like It, IV.i.32

So maybe you've followed the Bard's advice and taken a trip. Good. Now Shakespeare suggests there are good ways and bad ways to use your new worldy wisdom. Rosalind, a homebody and proud of it, makes fun of the bad way.

You know the type: they go to Italy for a week and return wearing their all-Gucci ensemble. After a heavily accented "Ciao bella!" and a kiss on both cheeks, they proceed to wax rhapsodic about the indescribable romance of their gondola ride, and to rail against how banal and uncultured we are here at home.

If Shakespeare traveled, he certainly never fell into this trap himself. Although he used foreign influences and settings to enrich his work, he was an English patriot who returned to his hometown to be buried in the same church where he was baptized. The Bard knew that we're products of our homeland. It shapes who we are, and if we're to be comfortable with ourselves we must be comfortable with our roots.

Shakespeare would fully approve of letting travel enrich you, but he had no patience for posers and complainers. If you've found someplace else that really makes you happier, he'd say please … move there.

What would Shakespeare do about pre-marital sex?

> ...Take my daughter.
> But if thou dost break her virgin-knot before
> All sanctimonious ceremonies may
> With full and holy rite be minist'red,
> No sweet aspersion shall the heavens let fall
> To make this contract grow; but barren hate,
> Sour-ey'd disdain, and discord shall bestrew
> The union of your bed with weeds so loathly
> That you shall hate it both.

Prospero, *The Tempest*, IV.i.14

Prospero is so protective of his daughter Miranda that he's kept her secluded with him throughout his long and lonely exile on an uninhabited island in the Mediterranean. But then along comes young Ferdinand, and it's love at first sight. "O brave new world," Miranda swoons, "that hath such creatures in it!" Prospero allows her and Ferdinand to marry, but not before pronouncing the above prohibition on pre-marital hoochie-coo.

Prospero's paternal strictures may well come from Shakespeare's own hard experience of the pitfalls of pre-marital sex. His eldest daughter, Susanna, was born six months after his marriage to local farmer's daughter Anne Hathaway. You do the math.

Whatever the reason, Shakespeare was a big proponent of the sanctity of marriage. Try counting the number of his comedies where the "happy ending" is a wedding, or a double wedding or, in the case of *A Midsummer Night's Dream*, even a triple wedding. And for a cautionary counterpoint, just look at how the young elopers Romeo and Juliet end up! Eternally in love, sure, but also quite dead.

What would Shakespeare do about marrying young?

A young man married is a man that's marred.

Parolles, *All's Well That Ends Well*, II.iii.298

Shakespeare should know something about marrying young, having tied the knot with Anne Hathaway at the tender age of 18. But what kind of marriage could it really have been, with Will working in London, obsessed with his Dark Lady mistress?

Although people are marrying later these days, I still see plenty of lives damaged by marrying too young. One of my best childhood friends was a talented actor who married right out of high school. He supported his wife while she continued her education, with the understanding that when she was done, he would go back to study theater. Well, her education took longer than planned, two kids happened, and the last time I saw him, fifteen years later, he was miserably managing the same restaurant where he used to wait tables in high school. His acting talent never saw the light of day.

Life, they say, is short; but a life marred by marrying too young can seem interminable. I know I wasn't mature enough to marry until well into my thirties. I suspect few people are. Shakespeare's sage advice: before you tie the knot, make sure you're old enough to tie your shoes.

Pillars of the State

Shakespeare loved politics. With access to the court of Queen Elizabeth, where many of his plays were first performed, and moving in the social circles of his patron the Earl of Southampton, the Bard had ample opportunity to glimpse the inner workings of state first hand. His examinations of the nature of political power treat not only the history of the English monarchy, but ancient civilizations as well.

But what place do Shakespeare's political/historical musings have here, in a book devoted to personal development? I was hoping you'd ask.

Too often self-help literature is truly selfish, focusing only on the needs of the individual. For the Bard, the individual was merely a small part of the great chain of being, from family to village, from village to town, and so on to county, nation, world, universe. The health of the entire chain is essential for the health of the individual. How can we be happy, fulfilled, fully-realized individuals, if the state we live in is diseased? Shakespeare knew this, and passed along his wisdom for how we can and should improve our lives by being informed, active, and thoughtful members of the community at large.

What would Shakespeare do to learn from history?

> There is a history in all men's lives,
> Figuring the nature of the times deceased;
> The which observed, a man may prophesy,
> With a near aim, of the main chance of things
> As yet not come to life.
>
> Warwick, *Henry IV Part Two*, III.i.80

It is said that those who do not learn from their mistakes are doomed to repeat them. Here, Richard II has predicted that Lord Percy would one day betray the usurper Bolingbroke; Percy had already betrayed Richard, so it was easy enough to predict he'd do it again. Shakespeare observer of human nature, but he also hints that we should use our intellect and reason to examine the greater flow of history, the "nature of times deceased" to shape our own ends.

The Bard's portrayals of Bronze Age Greece (*Troilus and Cressida*), Republican Rome (*Julius Caesar*) and Ptolemaic Egypt *(Antony and Cleopatra)* suggest these great ancient civilizations' fatal flaws. All rose to glory but fell under the weight of their own greed, ambition and short-sightedness. Each believed they were beyond the reach of history and yet their ends, in historical perspective, were inevitable.

Shakespeare's dissection of his own recent English history indicates he was constantly working to keep Elizabeth's England from going down the same ruinous path. The Bard urges us to learn from our own experiences to improve our lives and from the lessons of history to improve our society.

What would Shakespeare do about the social order?

> *The heavens themselves, the planets and this centre*
> *Observe degree, priority and place ...*
> *How could ...*
> *The primogenity and due of birth,*
> *Prerogative of age, crowns, sceptres, laurels,*
> *But by degree, stand in authentic place?*
> *Take but degree away, untune that string,*
> *And, hark, what discord follows!*

> Ulysses, *Troilus and Cressida*, I.iii.85

The great Ulysses rails against the social disarray which must surely come when "degree, priority and place" are not observed. Shakespeare comes across as a strict conservative, championing the medieval social order: from King of Heaven to King of England down through nobles and merchants all the way down to lowly peasants, who oughta be damn happy they have a place at all.

Many take Ulysses' view as Shakespeare's own. But hold on. *Troilus and Cressida* is one of Shakespeare's most brutally skeptical and cynical works. The play ends in chaos, with Ulysses' rigid order in a shambles.

Shakespeare was a big proponent of order, but with the Renaissance in full flower and the Copernican revolution just around the corner, perhaps Shakespeare was struggling with the old *medieval* order, and searching for a new vision of the universe, one where earth is not the "centre." I think Shakespeare would be amazed by our society, where democracy, individual liberty and artistic expression are—at least in word, if not yet always in deed—more valued than "prerogative of age, crowns and sceptres." But he would also be aware that the success of such a society depends on the enduring wisdom, tolerance and active participation of its individual members.

What would Shakespeare do about a President who inhaled?

> Presume not that I am the thing I was;
> For God doth know, so shall the world perceive,
> That I have turn'd away my former self;
> So will I those that kept me company.

King Henry V, *Henry IV Part Two*, V.v.56

In today's political climate, Shakespeare's Prince Hal could never get elected President. As a young Prince of Wales, Hal was bad to the bone, hanging out in bars and brothels with thieves and ruffians. Talk about skeletons in the closet!

But when Prince Hal becomes King Henry V, and his old drinkin' buddy Falstaff comes looking for a position at court, the King renounces his old life, his old friends, his old self. He transcends his seedy past and becomes Shakespeare's model monarch, the "mirror of all Christian kings." What's more, Shakespeare hints that Henry V flourishes at least in part *because of* the lessons learned in his wild youth.

The Bard suggests that a leader should be judged by present actions, not past indiscretions. We all make mistakes when we're young. Shakespeare did. I know I did. The question is, did we learn from them? Did our mistakes make us better people? And if we allow ourselves to learn from mistakes, shouldn't we also allow our leaders to learn from their mistakes ... and to grow greater because of them? The transformation of Prince Hal to Henry V shows us Shakespeare's answer.

What would Shakespeare do about racism?

> He hath disgraced me, and ... scorned my nation; and
> what's his reason? I am a Jew. Hath not a Jew eyes? Hath
> not a Jew hands, organs, dimensions, senses, affections,
> passions—fed with the same food, hurt with the same
> weapons, subject to the same diseases, healed by the same
> means, warmed and cooled by the same winter and
> summer, as a Christian is? If you prick us, do we not
> bleed? If you tickle us, do we not laugh? If you poison us,
> do we not die?

Shylock, *The Merchant of Venice*, III.i.54

Sigh. Here in the first decade of the twenty-first century, I feel like I really shouldn't have to regale you with Shakespeare's eloquent condemnation of anti-Semitism, and by extension, racism. Doesn't everyone know, by now, that these are very bad things? Sadly, no, not everyone does.

I'm half-Jewish; I'm also blond-haired and blue-eyed, which, I suppose, throws people off guard enough that they feel comfortable tossing around anti-Semitic remarks in front of me. I'm also privy to reverse Semitism sometimes, like the Jewish TV producer who, when I told him I was half Jewish, said, "Oh, *that* explains it! I always wondered how you could be such a funny writer, with a name like *Winfield*."

SIGH. Shakespeare has been called anti-Semitic for his portrayal of Shylock, but I don't buy it. Just re-read that passage above. I think the Bard had a progressive take on race relations, and I think he'd be disgusted that even four hundred years after his groundbreaking work, many people still judge others by the color of their skin or the sound of their name.

What would Shakespeare do about capital punishment?

> *The quality of mercy is not strain'd,*
> *It droppeth as a gentle rain from heaven*
> *Upon the place beneath. It is twice blest:*
> *It blesseth him that gives and him that takes ...*
> *It is an attribute to God himself;*
> *And earthly power doth then show likest God's*
> *When mercy seasons justice.*

Portia, *The Merchant of Venice*, IV.i.184

There are some passages where Shakespeare's characters take a much harder line than this, and argue against mercy when dispensing justice. But Portia's plea for the life of Antonio is one of the most compelling, heartfelt, and poetic speeches in all of Shakespeare; to me, it has the ring of personal conviction. Perhaps I'm just projecting my own opinions onto the Immortal Bard here (probably for the last time!), but I believe Shakespeare would oppose the death penalty.

With more and more cases coming to light every day where new DNA evidence exonerates convicted criminals, we are learning that justice is never absolute. Yet the death penalty is the most absolute of punishments. Shakespeare would have been witness to public executions of unimaginable cruelty: beheadings, pressings, drawings and quarterings, hearts ripped out and shown still beating to the condemned. But we've come a long way in 400 years. I think that "Gentle William Shakespeare," in his compassion and humanity, would urge us to take the final step and let the gentle rain of mercy wash away all of our gallows and gas chambers and lethal-injection gurneys.

What would Shakespeare do about gun control?

> *How oft the sight of means to do ill deeds*
> *Makes ill deeds done.*
>
> *King John*, IV.ii.219

I was going to write a bit here about how this quote applies to dieting or smoking. Something like, "don't keep cigarettes around the house, it'll be easier to quit; throw out the potato chips, you won't snack on 'em." But the next lines in the same passage give it a much more serious cast:

> *Hadst not thou been by,*
> *…This murther had not come into my mind;*
> *But … finding thee fit for bloody villainy,*
> *Apt, liable to be employed in danger …*

So instead I'm going to project my opinion on the Bard one last time (really!) and assert that he's talking about gun control. He notes "how oft" ill deeds are done when the means are readily at hand; Shakespeare was clearly familiar with the statistics indicating that a gun in the home is four times more likely to be used against a family member than against an intruder. "Hadst thou not been by, this murther had not come into my mind"; he's obviously suggesting that a gun in the bedside drawer is simply too easy a weapon to grab in a fit of domestic anger, with tragic results.

Yep, no doubt about it. The Bard clearly advises us not to keep firearms around the house.

What would Shakespeare do to have compassion for the poor ... or the rich?

> Whiles I am a beggar, I will rail,
> And say there is no sin but to be rich;
> And being rich, my virtue then shall be
> To say there is no vice but beggary.

King John, II.i.593

There was a time during my college days when I'd have to scrabble to get together $1.25 for my one meal a day: a slice of pizza and a Coke at the local pizzeria. At the time, I called myself an anarchist and was fond of saying things like "eat the rich!" (I guess those slices of pizza weren't fulfilling my nutritional requirements.)

Nowadays, I'm well-off enough to order an entire pizza at a time, and I've become much more conservative—a liberal Democrat. Yet even I catch myself sometimes thinking, "Why don't poor people just get jobs? *I* did." How smug and elitist is *that*?

King John is a nasty character, but even he seems to realize that such polarization of rich and poor is a cynical exercise. Shakespeare saw the noble and the base in characters both rich and poor. He suggests that we should all treat each other with respect, neither coveting each other's riches nor being resentful of each other's needs, and let our actions and our integrity, not the size of our wallets, proclaim our virtue.

What would Shakespeare do about hypocritical lawgivers?

> *Thou rascal beadle, hold thy bloody hand!*
> *Why dost thou lash that whore? Strip thine own back;*
> *Thou hotly lust'st to use her in that kind*
> *For which thou whipp'st her.*

King Lear, IV.vi.160

Shakespeare had a keen eye and a sharp tongue for hypocrisy of all sorts. Here, Lear, who is old and slightly mad and telling it like it is, berates the "beadle" (a local enforcement officer) for desiring the same prostitute he would punish. One can't help but think of thrice-divorced Congressmen extolling family values, or the mayor caught patronizing the very same strip club he's trying to run out of town.

It happens all the time, yet in our day as in Shakespeare's we buy into the pitches of politicians who make their living railing on and legislating against others' all-too-human vices. Lear sees this hypocrisy for what it is; so should we. To borrow a couple of phrases from other "What Would ___ Do?" territory: let he who is free from sin cast the first stone. Judge ye not, that ye be not judged. This bit of wisdom from the New Testament—which is among that good book's most oft-ignored strictures—is one Shakespeare urges us to heed.

What would Shakespeare do about the homeless?

> *Poor naked wretches, whereso'er you are,*
> *That bide the pelting of this pitiless storm,*
> *How shall your houseless heads and unfed sides,*
> *Your loop'd and window'd raggedness, defend you*
> *From seasons such as these? O, I have ta'en*
> *Too little care of this! Take physic, pomp;*
> *Expose thyself to feel what wretches feel,*
> *That thou mayst shake the superflux to them,*
> *And show the heavens more just.*

King Lear, III.iv.28

Aging King Lear, evicted from his ungrateful daughters' homes, learns firsthand what it's like to be homeless and caught out in a storm. The experience moves him to call on the powerful and wealthy to take a dose of the same medicine ("take physic, pomp")—in order to gain a compassion for the unhoused and unfed. Then he suggests that the rich give their superfluous wealth to the homeless as a sign of heavenly justice.

As an indication of his compassion and generosity, Shakespeare himself left a hefty bequest to "the poore of Stratford" in his will. He obviously took seriously the responsibility of housing and feeding those less fortunate than ourselves, and he'd surely urge us to do the same.

One can't help but wonder: if our presidents and prime ministers took Lear's invitation and each spent a single night, homeless, in a storm ... would the problem of homelessness disappear?

What would Shakespeare do about preachers who preach intolerance?

> Mark you this, Bassanio,
> The devil can cite Scripture for his purpose.
> An evil soul producing holy witness
> Is like a villain with a smiling cheek,
> A goodly apple rotten at the heart.
> O, what a goodly outside falsehood hath!

Antonio, The Merchant of Venice, I.iii.98

I may get my book boycotted for saying this, but I get really cranky when people who claim to be spreading the gospel of universal brotherhood and love for all humankind dig up bits of ancient scriptural law as justification for fatwahs or holy wars or such barbaric pronouncements as "homosexuality is an abomination" or "capital punishment is God's will."

Shakespeare, like nearly all Elizabethans, considered himself a Christian, and yet this passage clearly suggests he would have frowned upon such a rigid and self-serving interpretation of Scripture. The Bard always had a deep and abiding suspicion of the "holier-than-thou" type, like Hamlet's "ungracious pastor" who preaches "the steep and thorny road to heaven, whiles ... he the primrose path of dalliance treads." Shakespeare had too much sympathy for our flawed human nature to heed such rotten-hearted condemnations of one human being by another; he'd urge us to beware of such intolerant "evil souls."

What would Shakespeare do about defense spending?

> *Peace itself should not so dull a kingdom ...*
> *But that defenses, musters, preparations*
> *Should be maintained, assembled, and collected,*
> *As were a war in expectation.*

The Dauphin of France, *Henry V*, II.iv.16

Even the effete and ineffectual Dauphin of France, whose forces get slaughtered by the "warlike Harry" in England's victory at Agincourt, pronounces this doctrine of military preparedness clearly. Too bad his troops weren't as prepared as he himself suggests they should be!

You've guessed by now that I'm no warmonger. But in Shakespeare's England, military preparedness was essential because her monarch was a woman, and thus thought by the other monarchs of Europe to be an easy target for invasion. But readiness and cunning allowed Queen Elizabeth I to defeat the "invincible" Spanish Armada, and England to become the dominant world power of her day.

Shakespeare knew that any nation as envied as Elizabeth's England should be prepared for war at all times, the better to avoid it. I suspect his counsel would be unchanged today.

What would Shakespeare do about fighting?

> *Beware*
> *Of entrance to a quarrel; but being in,*
> *Bear't that th'opposed may beware of thee.*

Polonius, Hamlet, III.i.65

Having lost an admired contemporary playwright (Christopher Marlowe) to a stab wound resulting from a barroom brawl over a dinner bill, Shakespeare knew that even the tiniest conflict can quickly turn deadly. The Bard also reminds us that even entering a quarrel with good intentions can go awry. In *Romeo and Juliet*, when a high-on-love Romeo steps into the middle of a duel, his friend Mercutio ends up mortally wounded and wondering plaintively of Romeo, "Why the devil came you between us?"

The advice applies to conflicts between nations as well. There are clearly conflicts in Shakespeare's history plays that he considers justified—when combatting oppression, for example, as in the defeat of the tyrant Richard III at Bosworth Field. Other times, wars are clearly capricious, as in the Irish campaigns of Richard II that lead to Bolingbroke's rebellion. (As for Henry V's wars against France? In Shakespeare's day, any opportunity to beat up the French was seemingly justification enough!)

Shakespeare would have us use our reason and intellect to determine which quarrels are just. Polonius's admonition shows he would have us err on the side of non-intervention, but once engaged in a quarrel, have our enemy truly fear us.

What would Shakespeare do to honor a veteran?

> *[Have] pity of mine age, whose youth was spent*
> *In dangerous wars whilst you securely slept.*

Titus Andronicus, III.i.2

The many indignities that pepper the gory tale of Titus Andronicus and his family—rape, murder, mutilation, cannibalism (I love this play!)—all stem from one sad inciting incident: Titus, who gave his life in service as a Roman general, gets nothing but dissed for his pains.

I'm one of the lucky ones; I have truly "slept securely" my whole adult life. Wars have been distant, far-off events, thanks largely to the generations before me who went to war in darker times. As I said, I'm no warmonger. But I am nothing if not grateful to those who have done the nasty business of fighting wars against tyranny and oppression so that I haven't had to.

Shakespeare seems to have been of like mind. There are no records of his fighting in his country's wars, but he was intensely patriotic. He honored the memories of those who fought and died for England with his most heroic verse. And his sad tale of *Titus Andronicus* reminds us that regardless of how we feel about the justness of a particular war, or war in general, we should take care of our veterans.

The Undiscover'd Country

Finally we get to the Big Questions: death, fate, God, the afterlife. Shakespeare, like most of us, was fascinated with the unknown, and especially the afterlife, "the undiscover'd country, from whose bourne no traveler returns." We all want to know where we come from, why we're here, where we're going.

But it's no simple task, finding Shakespeare's "answers" to these questions. He wrote about so many different cultures and religions, from such a tolerant, almost neutral point of view, that it's difficult to separate his own feelings about the great mysteries of life from those of the characters he created.

But I've come too far to bail out on you now. I'll go ahead and ask, "What's it all about, Willy?"

I think you'll find that in these last pages, we gain an image of Shakespeare as a man asking the great questions but ultimately finding just small answers, in the simple truths of our poignantly transient human lives. And that's exactly why it's appropriate to keep asking ourselves, "What would Shakespeare do?" and carefully consider our answers. Because it turns out that those tiny choices we make every day of lives, those small decisions about our friends and enemies, our spouses and children, our lovers, our fellow human beings—aren't small at all, but are immeasurably profound.

What would Shakespeare do about submitting to God's will?

> *Here on this molehill will I sit me down.*
> *To whom God will, there be the victory!*
> *For Margaret my Queen, and Clifford too,*
> *Have chid me from the battle; swearing both*
> *They prosper best of all when I am thence.*
> *Would I were dead, if God's good will were so.*
>
> *Henry VI Part Three*, II.v.14

Although Shakespeare would almost certainly have considered himself a religious man, he seems not to have looked favorably on those who surrender completely to "God's will."

Henry VI is perhaps the most pious of Shakespeare's kings. He invokes the name of God seemingly every other line. And yet Henry VI is also perhaps the least ... well, *kingly* of kings. The image of him here—sitting on a molehill, having been told by his queen to take a powder because he's no help on the battlefield—is almost comical. Okay, so maybe his piety guarantees him a spot in heaven, but what about all the soldiers and innocents who die in the war that his feeble kingship is powerless to prevent? Are their souls on his tab?

Shakespeare always urges us to be strong, to take personal responsibility for our lives. In the Bard's universe, weakly trusting in God's good will alone may leave you, like a certain King Henry, sitting pathetically on the molehill of history.

What would Shakespeare do if he needed a miracle?

> *Miracles are ceased;*
> *And therefore we must needs admit the means*
> *How things are perfected.*

Canterbury, *Henry V*, I.i.67

Henry V makes that extraordinary turnaround from wastrel to "the mirror of Christian kings." But a figure no less than the Archbishop of Canterbury says his transformation is no miracle; that there were worldly "means" to account for his royal perfection.

Shakespeare's comedies and tragedies are full of miracles, big and small: ghosts, fairies, prophetic dreams, divine interventions. But when it comes to the history plays, which examine real people under the overarching theme of "what are the attributes of a good king?" miracles are few and far between. His monarchs are human beings whose rise or fall depends not on miracles but on their wisdom and valor.

Shakespeare indicates that we need neither thank nor blame a divine power for all of our successes and failures, but look to our own actions. When an athlete makes a spectacular leaping catch to win a game and then thanks the Lord for the miracle, I often find myself saying, "Dude, give yourself a *little* credit. The Lord isn't the one waking up, running five miles and hitting the weight room before practice every morning." I think Shakespeare would say the same.

What would Shakespeare do to see things as they really are?

> The cloud-capp'd towers, the gorgeous palaces,
> The solemn temples, the great globe itself,
> Yea, all which it inherit, shall dissolve,
> And like this insubstantial pageant faded
> Leave not a rack behind. We are such stuff
> As dreams are made on; and our little life
> Is rounded with a sleep.

Prospero, The Tempest, IV.i.152

Prospero, a character often said to be modeled on Shakespeare himself, posits a poignant vision of the physical world as transient, illusory, a dream wherein all those things that seem to us most substantial will fade, leaving not the wisp of a cloud behind. And what comes after this life? Prospero, a magician deeply learned in the mysteries of the universe, hints that it is only a "sleep."

What can we glean from this? In a world where all things must ultimately fade, where there is no assured afterlife, what can we hold on to? The resolution of Prospero's story suggests an answer. From bitter, banished recluse, living in a supernatural world of his own construction, Prospero finally renounces his magic to return home to the real world, to see his daughter wed, and then retire to Milan where, he says, "every third thought shall be my grave." Shakespeare would have us enjoy the small pleasures of our "little lives" while we can: our children, our friends, a peaceful retirement. These intangible treasures are what we should value, because the tangible ones are no more substantial than a dream.

What would Shakespeare do when contemplating the afterlife?

> To die, to sleep;
> To sleep, perchance to dream. Ay, there's the rub.
> For in that sleep of death what dreams may come
> When we have shuffl'd off this mortal coil
> Must give us pause.

Hamlet, III.i.63

This passage from Hamlet's megafamous "To be or not to be" speech, wherein Hamlet contemplates suicide, hints at what seems to be Shakespeare's genuine apprehension about death. The Bard's visions of the afterlife are jumbled and tormented. Hamlet darkly imagines the troubled dreams that might visit us in the "sleep of death." Angelo, in *Measure for Measure*, contemplates what it will be like "to lie in cold obstruction and to rot." In the Sonnets, the Bard contemplates what it will be like "with vilest worms to dwell." I can't help thinking that if he were alive today, he'd be into the whole Goth thing, writing plays like *Much Ado About Plasma* and *The Draining of the Shrew*.

Shakespeare may never have resolved his fears and doubts about "the undiscover'd country"; the afterlife is, after all, the greatest mystery of our existence, and likely to remain so. But Shakespeare's fear of death also produced in him its corollary, an appreciation of life. For Hamlet, it's a healthy respect for death that keeps him from suicide. The Bard would have us face the uncertainty of the afterlife full-on. He pleads with us to live each day of our brief lives as if it were our last, "to love that well, which thou must leave ere long."

What would Shakespeare do when facing death?

> *There is a special providence in the fall of a sparrow. If it*
> *be now, 'tis not to come; if it be not to come, it will be now;*
> *if it be not now, yet it will come. The readiness is all.*

Hamlet, V.ii.219

Shakespeare believed that we are generally the masters of our fate. That, as Hamlet puts it, we may "rough-hew" our lives how we will. But the simple resignation of Hamlet's line here, as he faces his final and fatal duel with Laertes, indicates the Bard believed that when our time's up, it's up. After all of Hamlet's dark ruminations on death, this comes across as a surprisingly accepting attitude towards mortality.

Interestingly, it's only when Hamlet comes to this point of acceptance that he can accomplish the task he set himself in Act I: avenging his father's murder. Shakespeare seems to be saying we must come to terms with the inevitability of our own death in order to have clarity and serenity in life.

I think Shakespeare would be amused by our obsession with long life—vitamins, low-fat diets, blood replacement, genetics, cryogenic freezing—do what you will, the ending is the same for all of us sparrows. As Caesar says, "cowards die many times before their deaths, the valiant never taste of death but once." Good Master Shakespeare advises us to be valiant, face death, and live life to its fullest, now, today, this very moment.

What would Shakespeare do to cheat death?

Not marble nor the gilded monuments
Of princes shall outlive this powerful rhyme.

Sonnet #55

This is, for me, one of the great beauties of Shakespeare's work. The Bard was haunted by images of all-devouring Time and a dark, decaying death. But throughout his most personal writings (the 154 sonnets) he expresses the hope that even if all else must fade—brass, lofty towers, gates of steel—he hopes and believes that at least his love will live on, because it is expressed in his "eternal lines" of verse. How wonderful and extraordinary is it that Shakespeare's fondest wish came true!? That he cheated death? That his verse does live on? That even today, we call him The Immortal Bard? I think it's one of the great triumphs of the human spirit, one that encourages us to follow our dreams no matter how high and unattainable they may seem.

I know what you're thinking: "I'm no Shakespeare. Heck, I'm not even a Stephen King or a John Grisham. I can't write a decent postcard, much less immortal literature!" Don't panic. Shakespeare saw another way to cheat death....

What would Shakespeare do to cheat death if he wasn't Shakespeare?

> *If ten of thine ten times refigur'd thee,*
> *Then what could death do if thou shouldst depart,*
> *Leaving thee living in posterity?*
> *Be not self-will'd, for thou art too much fair*
> *To be death's conquest, and make worms thine heir.*

Sonnet #6

For Shakespeare, there were two ways to defeat "the bloody tyrant Time" and outlive this life. One was by writing immortal verse. But for those of us who aren't Bards of the Ages, he offered another route, which he considered a way "more blessed than my barren rhyme." Have children. Whether or not you choose to have ten, as Shakespeare proposes to his young patron, Will clearly saw procreation as the simplest path to immortality.

But I'm going to go one step beyond Shakespeare. I don't believe, as Mark Antony says of Caesar, "that the evil men do lives after them, but the good is oft interred with their bones." I think the good we do in this life lives just as long as immortal verse or fair-faced progeny. I think our good deeds have a way of spreading outward like ripples in a pond to create good in the lives of others, some as yet unborn. I would argue that simply by living our lives with as much generosity and kindness as we can, and by being a positive influence on the lives of others, we all achieve immortality.

I don't think the Bard would disagree; and immortal as his *verse* may be, he ain't around to argue the point.

What would Shakespeare do about finding religion?

> *I commend my soul into the hands of God my Creator*
> *hoping & assuredly believing through the only merits of*
> *Jesus Christ my Savior to be made partaker of life*
> *everlasting and my body to the Earth whereof it is made.*

Shakespeare's Will

The Bard writes so credibly and non-judgmentally about ancient Greeks and their gods, ancient Romans and theirs, pre-Christian Britons and theirs, the Jew Shylock and his, one almost begins to suspect that Shakespeare, during his career, had no deep and abiding faith. Perhaps that's why he had such apprehension about the afterlife. But then, in a will written just a month before his death, he commends his soul to Christ. Perhaps Shakespeare finally made his peace with death ... and *his* God.

Shakespeare's works are notable for what Samuel Coleridge called his "wonderful philosophic impartiality." What matters to Shakespeare the poet and playwright is not what faith or belief an *individual* professes, but that the human race as a whole has a compelling desire to celebrate the wonder of the universe through ritual and worship. Regardless of what our own religious beliefs may be, we can all take a cue from the Bard, who was always questioning and searching, perhaps finding comfort in his own religious beliefs, while simultaneously respecting and learning from the diverse beliefs of his fellow human beings.

What would Shakespeare do with a bug?

> *The poor beetle that we tread upon*
> *In corporal sufferance finds a pang as great*
> *As when a giant dies.*

Isabel, Measure for Measure, III.i.78

Such a small question, when we're dealing with such Big Issues as death, God, fate and the afterlife. Yet in many ways, this is the biggest philosophical question of them all. If gentle William Shakespeare was truly a figure of compassion, if he believed that our character is not only revealed but actually *built* through our actions in the smallest of everyday circumstances, then what he would do with a beetle becomes a very, very heavy question.

Now I'm not saying Shakespeare never squished a bug. But I like to think he'd hesitate to send even the smallest creature headlong into that fearsome "undiscover'd country." Mind you, I'm no fanatic. If that fly is driving me crazy, and refuses to fly out of the open window I've offered it, I'll swat it. And don't get me started on mosquitoes ... nasty little bloodsuckers....

But that spider scurrying across the table? Who's it hurting? Do you need to kill it? Why not get a glass and a piece of junk mail, catch the little guy and put him outside? Who knows, maybe he'll repay the kindness and eat one of those nasty mosquitoes for you.

The universe works that way, sometimes.

What would Shakespeare do above all?

> *This above all: to thine own self be true,*
> *And it must follow, as the night the day,*
> *Thou canst not be false to any man.*

Polonius, Hamlet, I.iii.78

Kinda says it all.

That William Shakespeare, he had a way with words, didn't he?

Further Reading

If by chance this little book has piqued or revived your interest in Shakespeare's works and you'd like to read more, you're in luck. William Shakespeare is the most written-about figure in the history of literature. These suggestions will only skim the surface.

The best place to begin is with Shakespeare's works themselves. But if possible, don't read them! Shakespeare was meant to be seen and heard, not read. A good live production will draw out meanings and subtleties that you might miss in a hundred readings of the same play.

For reading the Bard's works, find a good annotated edition—one where the footnotes are on the same page as the text (nothing's more frustrating than constantly flipping to the back of the book for a gloss). Both the Arden and Oxford individual editions are all of high quality, with illuminating footnotes.

If you're new to Shakespeare and want recommendations for which plays to try first, I'd suggest starting out with *A Midsummer Night's Dream*, *Julius Caesar*, *Macbeth*, and of course *Romeo and Juliet*, then move on to the great tragedies like *Hamlet* and *King Lear*. For an unusual lesser-known play, try *Cymbeline*. It has elements of comedy, history, tragedy, and romance, all lumped into one sprawling heap.

For a fun, fast, tongue-in-cheek intro to the Bard's whole canon, why not pick up the breezy and very popular paperback of *The Reduced Shakespeare Company's Complete Works of William Shakespeare (abridged)*, co-written and edited by yours truly (New York: Applause Books, 1993). You can read it in an afternoon and say you've read the Complete Works. Plus, I'll get a royalty!

For a more serious Complete Works edition, I stand by my trusty copy of *The Riverside Shakespeare*, edited by G. Blakemore Evans

(Boston: Houghton Mifflin Company, 1974). It includes great footnotes, a biography, timeline, facsimile pages from the First Folio, contemporary records and allusions to Shakespeare, historical background info, discussions of Elizabethan theater ... in short, everything anyone aside from serious Shakespeare scholars would need to know about the Bard. It's also number one on my list of Desert Island Books.

There are hundreds of biographies of Shakespeare. Be careful. All are largely conjectural and many are written by loonies and will turn out to be biographies of Christopher Marlowe or Edward DeVere! Most decent editions of the plays will have a sufficient biography. If you ache for more, try *William Shakespeare—A Compact Documentary Life* by Samuel Schoenbaum, (New York: Oxford University Press, 1987) for a nothing-but-the-facts approach, or A. L. Rowse's *Shakespeare the Man* (New York: St. Martin's Press, 1973) for a good blend of well-rendered fact and not-improbable guesswork.

For a balanced investigation of the historical evidence about Shakespeare that doesn't rule out the possibility that someone else wrote "his" works, I'd suggest *Shakespeare: The Evidence*, by Ian Wilson (New York: St. Martin's Griffin, 1993).

For a delightfully entertaining fictional account of Shakespeare's love life, treat yourself to Anthony Burgess' *Nothing Like the Sun* (New York: W.W. Norton and Company, 1996).

For a dry literary companion guide to the Works, there's *The Cambridge Companion to Shakespeare Studies*, edited by Stanley Wells (Cambridge University Press, 1986).

But if you're like me, you'll be more interested in the classic guide to everything sexual in Shakespeare (and there's more than you'd think possible): *Shakespeare's Bawdy*, by Eric Partridge (New York and London: Routledge, 1947).

Because of Shakespeare's status as the greatest uncopyrighted writer ever, there is also a tremendous amount of material freely available on the Internet. A good starting place is Terry Gray's *Mr. William Shakespeare and the Internet*, at http://daphne.palomar.edu/shakespeare, with extensive content of their own and an easily-navigable, intuitive set of links to other sites.

There are two great online compilations of the Complete Works, where you can search the plays by character, word, phrase—you name it. The best-designed and most thorough is Jeremy Hylton's *Shakespeare MIT* site at http://tech-two.mit.edu/Shakespeare, but the most reliable search engine is found at Matty Farrow's *The Works of the Bard* at www.gh.cs.su.oz.au/~matty/Shakespeare/Shakespeare.html.

If you want to amuse yourself by hearing people who think Shakespeare wrote Shakespeare (Stratfordians) lob the latest personal attacks against those who don't (Marlovians and Oxfordians) and vice versa, there's a fountain of misinformation and flawed reasoning on the humanities.lit.authors.shakespeare Usenet newsgroup. There are also some genuine Shakespeare scholars there, some terrific discussion, and an excellent FAQ.

And finally, in keeping with Shakespeare's practicality, if you read the bit about sound financial planning and investing and want to know more, what better place to start than the Shakespeare-tinged finance site *The Motley Fool*, at www.fool.com. They know that a wise man knows he is a fool, and will get you on the right financial track with their 13 Steps to Foolish Investing.

JESS WINFIELD co-founded the Reduced Shakespeare Company and is co-author of *The Complete Works of William Shakespeare (abridged)*, the longest-running (four-years) comedy in London's West End. He also directed the off-Broadway production of the play and edited (under the fraudulent pseudonym J. M. Winfield) a farcically annotated version of it for print publication. A writer and story editor for the Walt Disney Company (where he's worked on, among other things, *Buzz Lightyear of Star Command*, *101 Dalmations*, Emmy-nominated *Disney's Mickey Mouseworks*, adaptations of "The Tempest" and "A Midsummer Night's Dream," and an animated feature with the formidible title "The Incredible Almost True Life Story of Young William Shakespeare and a Muse Named Bob"), Jess lives in Los Angeles.